Praise for Linda Lynch and <u>The Executive Guide to Trouble Free IT</u>

"Finally, an expert has taken the time to explain the ABC's of the most powerful revolution in modern corporate America. Moving us from chronic emergencies to expansive productivity, this manual is a must read for those of us who are bewildered by the jargon, don't know the questions to ask, and who seek some sanity in this complex world of communication."

Wendell W. Parsons, CEO
Stamprite Supersine

"As I read Linda's book, I discovered that I do not know as much about technology as I need to. The information in her book will help me save my business both time and money as we make technology decisions."

Chuck Levy, President
Shinberg Insurance Services

"In <u>The Executive Guide to Trouble Free IT</u>, Linda clearly explains the seldom considered aspects of maintaining your information systems. She explains concepts at an executive level, allowing you to make informed IT management decisions. She gives many examples of how reputable companies deliver computer network management services. A vital read for anyone considering investing in their company's technology infrastructure!"

Fred Reck, President
InnoTek Computer Consulting, Inc.

"As the CEO of Medical Management Systems of Michigan, Inc. it is critical that I have an understanding and working knowledge of our IT infrastructure and can make decisions that connect our Business Plan with our technology investments and decisions. It is essential that I know how to obtain tangible business value from any IT investments that are made.

This book succeeds in providing valuable information and bridging the technology knowledge gap. Linda succeeds in taking complicated language and concepts and explaining them in a way that can be easily understood

Linda's book will allow the untrained, non-technology business person to have discussions and make decisions *with* their IT department or staff and not *in spite* of them. Her book provides information that will allow for more open and productive discussions between the business side, and the IT side, allowing these two critical aspects of most businesses to work together to meet the needs of the company.

I hope you find this book as enlightening and informative as I did."

Jeanne P. Rutledge, President
Medical Management Systems of Michigan, Inc.

"If you are in charge of making the technology decisions at your business this book is a must read! Linda explains the details of today's most common business technologies in a simple and straight forward manner. There is something for everyone in this book."

Ryan Doom, CEO
Web Ascender

"In her book, <u>The Executive Guide to Trouble Free IT</u>, Linda excels where so many others do not. She demystifies information technology to help any business owner understand how they can best leverage technology to help their company soar. So many businesses invest in technology without a clear plan or understanding of what they hope to accomplish. Linda does an exemplary job distilling the lingo of the technology industry, so that you may be an informed consumer and make good decisions. Throughout the book, Linda offers numerous practical tips to help you get the most from your technology. Along the way, she maps out a blueprint based on her years of experience and stature in the technology industry that will help any business ensure they are not just successful in the implementation of new technologies but that also in gaining a competitive advantage. Good reading!"

MJ Shoer, President and Virtual Chief Technology Officer
Jenaly Technology Group, Inc.

"As an executive, you need general knowledge so you can delegate to someone you trust to get the job done ASAP. We have had a fantastic experience with Linda and her team. Everyone breaks down the language to understandable English."

Ellen Weaver, Executive Director
Capital Area Center for Independent Living

"Linda's team functions just like another department within our organization, another employee. We have always considered them to be one of the best vendors we have, and certainly one of the oldest."

Joe Delbrocco, Vice President
Carpak Manufacturing, Inc.

The Executive Guide to Trouble Free IT

The Executive Guide to Trouble Free IT

Technology Basics Explained in Plain English

Linda J. Lynch

Harry —

Best wishes!

ISBN 978-0-9828432-0-8

Printed in the United States of America

Design by Tony Moore, Tony Moore Design

Photography by J. D. Small, J. D. Small Studios

To John

Table of Contents

Foreword

If you use a computer as a helpful tool, and not as a way of life, you may have experienced some confusion when faced with geek-speak; the jargon and terms repair technicians use when attempting to explain what went wrong. As with any new language, it's much easier to get by if you have an easy to read and understand guide.

This guide does not assume, as so many others do, that you have some innate understanding of computers and how they work. Linda Lynch knows computers inside and out, and one of her greatest strengths is that she also knows that you do not, so she starts explaining in easy to understand, plain English terms right from the beginning.

Follow along with Linda, as she takes you beyond the geek-speak to a basic understanding, giving you the confidence to make educated choices and decisions. If you've ever been frustrated with your computers or your network, this book is for you. New users and seasoned professionals alike will learn from Linda's vast experience helping thousands of people get more out of their technology.

David Snell, MCSE/MCDBA
President and Founder
ACTSmart, Inc.
American Computer Technologies
Marshfield, Massachusetts

Introduction

Time after time we sit down to talk to prospects and find that they feel as if they are being held hostage by their IT company. Many times they don't have the minimum information required to effectively administer their own network. Sometimes they don't even know how many servers they have or what function each of the servers in their network performs.

Whether you are a business owner, the CEO of a small company or the Executive Director or President of a non-profit, you are undoubtedly very good at leading your organization. After all, you can't manage to be successful any other way. I don't doubt that if I come to you for the services you provide, you might tell me things that at first confuse me because I am not familiar with the ins and outs of your industry. If you want to earn my trust and my business or my support, you will have to provide enough explanation in terms I can understand for me to be comfortable with my decision.

By the same token, you should expect the same thing from your IT company. You deserve all of the information about the pros and cons of each solution that is being proposed. I have never made an initial proposal to a client that wasn't a solution I would have implemented if I were running the company. Sometimes, the client asks about the costs to implement a more robust solution, and after discussing the increased cost and the additional benefits, we settle on a more expensive solution.

You should also expect that everything is explained in plain English. The explanation shouldn't include a lot of acronyms that aren't familiar to you, offered without any explanation.

Of course, this is all easier if you already have a little bit of knowledge. That's why I decided to write this book. While reading it won't make you an expert or able to support your network without one, it will make what you hear from your computer consultant and technicians a lot less baffling. You will also be able to ask the right questions to be sure you understand your technology decisions.

Linda Lynch
September 2010

Saving Money on Technology

None of us want to spend any more than we have to on much of anything. This chapter contains some tips that will help you get the most for your money when it comes to technology.

Tip Number 1 - Ask your computer support company to let you or your staff get involved with your project so you can learn to be more self-sufficient and shave off billable hours.

One of the best ways to save money on your computer support is to learn how to handle some of the basic, routine issues that arise in house. If you can be involved in the project you are outsourcing, it will go a long way to make you or your designated staff member competent to handle many of the small issues.

Many computer support companies will want to keep you as far away from your project as possible. After all, if you have to call them about every little issue, they will be able to bill you for more time. I don't think that is ethical and that is why we always try to involve our clients.

Let me illustrate this with a story: Recently, one of our clients was upgrading several machines in their office from Office 2003 to Office 2007. After loading files to the server, we needed to install the new software on a dozen machines. Since this particular client has a staff member whose responsibility is to provide first level support for all network issues, our technician showed her how to perform the upgrade. She was then able to perform the upgrades herself, saving billable hours and gaining valuable knowledge in the process.

We have been able to save other clients considerable money just by teaching them how to solve and fix problems while we are doing it. We also document everything we do for our clients in detail. All of the details are printed on the invoices and are available in our customer portal, allowing them to refer back to anything that has been done in the past.

Of course, not everyone wants to be involved at that level, and it's fine if you don't. Certainly if spending time on technology means you have less time to spend on activities that generate revenue or move your company forward, you probably don't want to get involved. But don't you think that should be a choice you make and not one that your computer support company makes for you? And your IT company's response to this request will tell you a lot about them, even if you don't ultimately take this approach.

Tip number 2 – Always ask for fixed pricing from your computer consultant.

This is an area where I see a lot of companies getting burned. Many computer support companies quote projects by giving an estimated cost to complete the project, but then also include an hourly rate that is added in for "unexpected" events that may arise during the project. Be very careful about signing this type of contract.

A competent computer network support company should have gathered enough information about your current situation, and should be familiar enough with the solution they are suggesting to know how many hours the project will require. They should be able to think through problems that could arise before they make their proposal. Tacking on an hourly rate and a clause that allows them to charge you for extra hours is a safety net for them. If their technician makes a mistake and takes longer than he or she should, or if they overlooked something when they put together the proposal, YOU will end up paying the price.

Before you know it, you are well into the project, the hours are adding up and the bill is far more than you were expecting. A dishonest computer support company might even give you a proposal with an impossibly low figure expecting to exceed it. That's why you should never make your decision based solely on the price you have been quoted.

Instead, asked for a fixed price quote or even a "not to exceed" proposal. If you can get a proposal that says the labor will not exceed a certain dollar amount, you may be billed less if the project goes smoothly. And if it doesn't, you will not be penalized.

Of course, if the computer support company is quoting you fixed fee or not to exceed, they may also lay out exactly what your responsibilities will be for the project in terms of making any necessary resources available and providing access to your equipment and office. Be sure that you understand what will be required of you and that you are not responsible for any delays or difficulties.

Tip number 3 – Never hire a computer support company without checking references.

You wouldn't hire a new employee without checking references, so why would you hire a computer support company without talking to a few of their recent clients? It would be particularly helpful if you talk to clients who have had similar problems or projects. If that's not possible, ask for clients who have done business with them consistently over at least a two year period.

This seems obvious, but a lot of companies skip this step. When you talk to their clients, be sure to ask the following questions:

- Did they deliver what they promised?
- Were they responsive and easy to get ahold of in times of emergency?
- Did they bill accurately?
- Did they stay within the projected budget?
- Would you use them again? Why or why not?

You might also ask if there were any problems that arose and how they handled them. Not every project goes as smoothly as one would like, and it isn't so much the problem as how the problem was handled when it happened. If the company you are talking to is hesitant to provide a list of clients, proceed with extreme caution.

You should also take advantage of Google searches and other online tools to find out what people are saying. Searching for the company's name will help you find comments made by other clients. You should also take note of any clients that are mentioned on their website and contact them as well.

If you use social networks, such as LinkedIn, Facebook or Twitter, search for mentions there as well, or simply ask your social network if anyone has done business with the company you are considering. Unless your network is small or the company you are talking to doesn't have very many clients, you are likely to get an opinion from someone.

Tip number 4 – Make sure you understand what you are getting from your IT company.

Every industry has its own jargon and information technology is certainly no exception - in fact, we may be one of the worst offenders!

If you don't understand the solution being proposed, then ask to have it explained to you in terms that you can understand. If the prospective computer support company can't do that, then don't hire them.

They should also be able to give you alternative solutions and educate you about the pros and cons of each solution. The best solution may not be the one that has the lowest upfront cost. Likewise a more expensive solution may have lots of additional features, but if they aren't features that will benefit you, you shouldn't spend the extra money.

A good computer support company will want to make sure you understand the decisions you are making. The very best companies will want you to make the decision that is the best one for you, even if it is not the most profitable one for them.

Don't be afraid to ask for explanations of terms or parts of the project in "layman's terms" if they aren't clear to you. Ask questions like "Tell me why this is absolutely necessary." or "What does that mean exactly?", or "Explain to me exactly how this will work once the project is completed."

If you are entering into a monthly contract for support services, be sure you understand what is included in the contract. Many providers have plans that range from budget to premium. The budget plan may include only monitoring, which means that you will be billed for any work done to resolve problems found as a result of the monitoring.

It is not unusual for premium plans to include unlimited time, but even these plans may not include everything. Some providers may specifically exclude labor required to set up new computers, quoting this work as a project, typically at a discounted rate. Others may be willing to include this type of work as part of the monthly fee, and some are even starting to include technology riders that provide for the replacement of every workstation in the network over the life of the contract.

Asking your IT company to be very specific will avoid expensive "misunderstandings" that can pop up in the middle of an issue putting you way over budget. And you certainly don't want to suddenly be receiving bills for additional services if you thought the monthly contract you signed was all-inclusive.

Tip number 5 – Get everything in writing for your technology project.

Once you are clear on the end result you want and how it is going to happen, get everything in writing to avoid confusion and disappointment further down the road. If your computer support company feels that particular goals are not achievable, then it is their responsibility to tell you so up front. By getting them to put everything in writing, you will be able to hold them accountable for the promises they make and responsible for outcomes not achieved.

Here are the details that you want to be sure are covered in your written agreement:

Confirm Payment Terms – This includes up front deposits, fee structure, and payments due on completion of the project. Most computer support companies will request an upfront deposit, particularly if your project includes the purchase of equipment. If the project is large, they may want additional payments based on the percentage of completion or reaching project milestones. For smaller projects, the balance may simply be due at installation.

Deliverables – Your written agreement should outline what you expect to be able to do when the project is done. You may need to include details about how the work should flow and what it should look like. Do not assume anything; if you expect it to happen, get it in writing as specifically as possible.

Work schedule and pace – Make sure you outline a date for completion. On larger projects, you will also want to specify dates for phases of delivery.

Again, any professional experienced computer support company will be more than happy to outline these items in writing prior to a project. If they hesitate or make excuses, it is a sign they are not confident in their ability to deliver on their promises.

Tip number 6 – Implement a rock solid backup plan.

You might be wondering how on earth a solid backup strategy will save you money. And if you don't ever have a failure it certainly won't appear to be money well spent.

But I have heard it said that there are two types of computer users - those who have had a hard drive crash and those who haven't - yet. The fact is that ALL hard drives eventually do fail and it is important that you are prepared when it happens to you.

There are many backup solutions available today. The most popular solutions are backups to hard drives that can be taken offsite or solutions that backup your data and send it offsite through the internet to a secure data center. Some of these solutions also have the ability to virtualize a failed server while you are waiting for repairs, reducing or even eliminating costly downtime.

If the computer support company you are interviewing or working with is still recommending that you backup to tape, you need to fire them immediately and find a company that is familiar with more

10

reliable backup solutions. Tape is the least reliable backup solution available today.

See the chapter on backups for an understanding of the key things you should be evaluating when you consider a backup solution.

Tip number 7 – Do business with "one-man-band" computer consultants carefully.

We regularly talk to prospects who have been doing business with a "one-man-band" and the relationship just isn't working out so well. Usually, it started out fine, but as time goes on, the "one man" is harder and harder to get in touch with, until finally he's not returning any of your phone calls.

Sometimes, the computer guy has a regular job and just does this on the side. Other times, he has lost his job, likes computers and thinks he can fix your problems. Or maybe he used to work for another computer support company and left because he thought he could make more money working for himself than he was getting paid before.

Typically, these guys charge a lot less than an established computer support company. I've even seen ads that say things like "I'll fix your computer for $40 labor – no matter how long it takes." That seems like a deal, but I'm guessing you would rather have someone who knows about how long it is going to take to fix your problem and quotes your job accordingly.

And when they stop taking your calls and don't call you back, they've either moved on to another job or state, or they don't have any idea how to solve your problems. Ignoring you seems like the best solution to their problem.

Even if you find a "one-man-band" that is competent and hasn't disappeared, what are you going to do when you have a problem and the one man is on vacation or tied up with another client who has a more serious problem?

Basically, as with all things in life, you get what you pay for. If you have mission critical applications and data that must be protected and working 24/7, then it makes sense to hire a well-established firm with a good track record and enough technicians on staff to quickly respond to any technical emergencies that arise.

What on Earth is Managed Services?

As you research IT companies looking for the one that is best qualified to provide IT services, you are likely to run across the term "Managed Services". That may leave you scratching your head and wondering just what that term means. IT companies actually do all of us a disservice when they throw out that term, which is largely meaningless on its own!

A managed service is basically any service where you pay a regular fee in return for some set of services. If you pay a pest control company to come to your home or office and spray for insects, you have subscribed to a managed service. You may contract for lawn service, snow removal or even routine maintenance on your heating and cooling system in the same way.

The key is in understanding exactly what services will be included in that monthly fee. If ABC Pest Control tells you that for $10 a month, they will spray for insects regularly and XYZ Bug Zappers tells you it will cost $25 a month for their service, which one will you pick? If that's all you know, you might just pick ABC, but if you ask a few questions you may find out that they aren't the same at all.

ABC sprays once a year. If you have a problem between scheduled applications, they will come out again, for the reduced fee of $45. (Without the service, a single application runs $75.) XYZ comes quarterly and if you have any problems between applications, or if they see any evidence of bugs when they spray, they will make additional applications at no additional charge. Now the choice is not as simple as it was based solely on price!

Unfortunately, what is included in a technology provider's managed services plan will vary greatly from company to company. In addition, most companies will have several plans that vary from a budget plan that provides only the most basic services to a premium "white glove" plan that is all-inclusive. But even if you are looking at

13

all-inclusive plans, you need to ask if there are items that would not be included in the all-inclusive plan!

Each company is likely to present their offerings in a way that is different from the others. The list below is a comprehensive list of services that could be included in a managed technology services plan.

Before you start into the list, be forewarned that it contains quite a few terms and acronyms that you may not be familiar with. Try as I might, I just couldn't figure out how eliminate them all without having pages and pages of information. Since they are likely to be terms you are going to hear as you interview technology companies, you will need to start to become familiar with them anyway. So, as you read through the list, you will notice that some of the terms are underlined. This indicates that they are explained further in the glossary.

- Virtual Chief Information Officer (CIO) Services
    - On-line Trouble Ticketing and Knowledgebase Access
    - Creation of Acceptable Use Policy (AUP)
    - Monthly Executive Reporting
    - Network Summary
    - Asset Reports
    - Annual Technology Planning Session
    - Quarterly Audit and Conference
    - Full Network Documentation
    - Virtual Chief Information Officer
    - Vendor Liaison
- Network Monitoring Services
    - Monitoring of Network, Servers and Desktops 24 x 7
        - Event and Error Logs
        - Hard Drive Space and Health
            - Automated Daily Cleanup
            - Automated Defragmentation
        - Exchange and SQL Database
        - Backup Processes Including Verification and Testing

- Other Services and Performance as Requested/Needed
  - o Advanced Support and Administration for Exchange and SQL
  - o Advanced Network Administration
  - o Policy Development and Enforcement
  - o User State Management
- Asset Tracking Services
  - o Hardware Asset and Configuration Management
  - o Software License Management
- Security Services / LAN Level
  - o Automated Microsoft Patch Management
  - o End Point Security – Anti-Virus, Anti-Spyware, Anti-Malware at the Desktop Level
- Backup / Disaster Recovery / Business Continuity
  - o Email Archiving
  - o Image Backup and Disaster Recovery of All Workstations
  - o Image Backup and Disaster Recovery of All Servers
  - o Offsite Data Backup
  - o Full Business Continuity Solution – Emergency Virtualization of Servers
- Website Hosting
- Security Services / WAN Level
  - o Hardware Firewall with Unified Threat Management (UTM)
  - o Gateway Anti-Virus and Anti-Spyware Protection
  - o External Anti-SPAM Protection
  - o Intrusion Prevention System
  - o Content and Application Filtering
  - o Bandwidth Management and VPN Support
  - o Internet Policy Management, Enforcement, Tracking and Reporting
  - o Real Time Reporting by Username and Group
- Hardware Replacement, Maintenance and Extended Warranty

- o Parts to Repair and Maintain Workstations, Notebooks and Servers Under Contract
  - o Emergency Loaner PCs or Servers
  - o Replacement of PCs and Notebooks During Life of Contract
- Support and Administration
  - o Help Desk
  - o Remote Support
  - o On-Site Support
  - o After Hours/Weekend Support

That's a long list, and if you have been dealing with your network and computers yourself, the chances are pretty good that you aren't doing many of those things, and maybe you aren't even really sure why some of them are important. Let me assure you that they are all important – if you want to be sure that your technology is functioning properly so that you can go about your business.

More than once, we've had clients who were on our premium "white glove" plan that decided to cut back on the service and ended up on the budget plan. Before you know it, employees are complaining that their systems are running slowly, there are problems with viruses and spyware and no one is happy. It is clear to me that regular maintenance is essential to a properly functioning office!

If your technology company is including all of these services in a monthly plan, they have shifted their focus from reacting to problems that you call them about, to being completely and totally focused on making sure, as much as possible, that your systems are all working properly. You see, if I am charging you a set amount each month, I will make more money by preventing problems, preferably while sitting in my office, than I can make by sending a technician to your office to fix a problem. Suddenly you and your technology partner are both benefiting from a network that functions properly!

How is this possible? Well, over the last several years, a variety of remote monitoring and maintenance tools have been developed that allow technology companies to keep track of what is going on with your workstations, servers and network without leaving their offices. These systems can be configured so that notifications are sent when anything happens that doesn't seem to be right – everything from networks that aren't connecting to the internet to errors on hard drives that appear to be running properly to issues with high memory or CPU utilization on your server.

When problems are observed, these same tools allow us to remotely login to your systems for further troubleshooting and remediation. Many times our clients are not even aware there has been a problem until they receive emails and reports letting them know what has happened.

When your employees have questions or problems, these same tools allow us to help them work through the issues. Our technicians remotely access the workstation and go through the steps with your employee. We can see exactly what they see, there is no miscommunication and problems are resolved very quickly.

Now admittedly not everything can be done remotely, but even when there is a problem that requires an onsite visit, it is typically much less stressful than it would be without these tools. For example, think about the last time you had a hard drive failure. You were hard at work when suddenly your system started making strange noises or just stopped responding to you at all. Or maybe you arrived in the morning, turned on your system and were greeted with "No Boot Device Found". You probably took your machine in for repair, or called your computer tech and waited for them to show up. Hopefully, they came prepared and you only lost a half a day of time, but wait – you didn't have a current backup? You had to start that proposal over again? AARGH!

If you were working with a company that was monitoring your systems, the chances are good (although not guaranteed) that the hard drive generated some errors to the event logs that indicated there was trouble ahead. You were contacted by the technician who set up a time to come out with a replacement drive. When the technician arrived, he copied all of the information on the failing drive to the new one and checked everything out to make sure there were no problems. You noticed right away that the system seemed faster (failing hard drives don't perform well) and you didn't lose any data. And even if the drive didn't give a warning (that happens sometimes), your IT company is keeping an image backup nightly and was able to completely restore your system to the way it was the night before the failure.

Budget or White Glove?

On a budget plan, you may get little more than monitoring, or perhaps monitoring and patching. The IT company you are working with will let you know that there is a problem and ask you if you would like them to fix it. Fixing problems will not be included and you will receive additional bills for the additional services. If security updates are included, you will at least know that your system is protected from attacks that take advantage of flaws in the operating system. While some might consider this to be proactive service, it really only serves to make the client the one who is forced to react instead of the IT company. If you are being told about a lot of problems, you may well wonder if the provider is making things up in order to generate additional revenue!

With an all-inclusive plan, you will pay one monthly fee and your technology partner will take care of everything for you. Problem with the copy machine not scanning to your network? Your IT company will troubleshoot the issue and contact the copy machine company if necessary. New cell phones? Not a problem – your technician will make sure that your email and calendar is syncing properly and even call the cell phone company to get answers to any questions. Internet down? Your technology partner will figure out if the problem is with the service entering the building or your equipment – and they will even do that on Saturday or Sunday!

But you do have to figure out just how all-inclusive the plan really is. Some companies may not include set up of new computers. If you get a new server, they may consider that to be a project and give you a price for configuring it and migrating to it from the old server. Your plan may or may not have a technology rider that provides for complete hardware warranty – everything from replacement of failed hard drives to complete workstations on a set schedule.

I'm not suggesting that a plan that places these restrictions is bad; I'm just pointing out that it is very important that you understand exactly what is and isn't included. If all of your computers are new, then it may not be of any value to you that the IT company will replace all of them on a schedule. If all of them are old, you may need all of them replaced up front. Maybe you have paid for extended warranties on all of your name brand computers, so even replacement of failed components doesn't matter. But if you are looking for one price that includes absolutely everything you need, make sure absolutely everything is really included!

What Does It Cost to be Down Anyway?

That's an excellent question. Obviously it depends on your specific situation, but you need to think about what your employees cost per hour – and don't forget that you are also paying taxes and providing benefits that add to the cost. Will those employees be able to  stay busy while you are waiting for problems to be resolved, or will you be paying them to sit and wait? Is customer service affected by downtime? What about revenue generation? If you are providing a professional service that requires use of the failed system, those hours are not recoverable.

In addition to the cost of idle employees and the lost revenue, there will be the cost of fixing the problem. Most often, problems that are found and fixed early are also fixed easily. When the initial problem is left unresolved, it typically escalates and the eventual solution becomes much more expensive. The hard drive scenario discussed earlier in this chapter is just one such example.

Proactive versus Reactive Service

As I finish this chapter, I'm reminded of one of the best stories I've recently observed to illustrate the benefits of contracting with a company that is really interested in providing proactive services.

In early 2009, we started working with Tomie Raines, Inc. Debbie Barnett, President and CEO, was unhappy because she seemed to be paying to fix the same problems over and over again. When we started working with her, there were surely a number of problems, the most serious involving Exchange and properly working email. Every user had been allowed to accumulate as much email as they wanted – and some had several years' worth of messages. That meant that Exchange was reaching the limits of total allowable mailbox space which caused it to be unstable and stop working often.

The outgoing company had come on-site and made minor changes which would get things working again, but never for more than a week or two. They had also proposed an upgrade to the server at a cost of $15,000 or so. Due to the economy, this wasn't a solution Barnett was in a position to consider.

When we took over, we too were initially making regular changes to keep things running, although we were able to make them remotely, and we were including this task in our monthly service plan – no additional billing for fixing this basic service. After we were able to investigate and understood the problem, we suggested that users be told that there would be limits on how much email they could save. The situation and the proposed limits were explained, users were given time to

clean up their email, and then the limits were set. The problems ceased and we were no longer spending time resolving them. And email delivery was once again reliable.

Barnett received the benefit of email that worked and a reduction in the amount of money being spent to fix it – and it didn't cost $15,000 to do it! We began spending our time addressing other issues to make even more improvements to the network.

The bottom line is that when we make things run more smoothly, we don't have to deal with as many emergencies and our clients are more productive. Hopefully we are both making more money!

What about HaaS and TaaS?

You may be working with a technology company that is proposing a HaaS or TaaS solution. These acronyms stand for Hardware as a Service and Technology as a Service respectively.

Both of these terms refer to an extension of monthly service plans that include the hardware necessary to run your business. If you enter into an agreement for HaaS, your provider will provide necessary hardware and software for each of your users. The agreement may also include the servers that are necessary to support them. If it is a TaaS agreement, then it will almost certainly include the servers and any other equipment that is necessary to make your network function properly.

Under this type of agreement, the hardware will belong to your provider and not to you. This will be the perfect solution for some companies as it eliminates capital expenditures in favor of operating expenses. It also eliminates the upfront cost of purchasing technology and preserves cash for activities that are more directly related to generating revenue. This type of arrangement also makes it easy to increase or decrease the number of users as your situation changes, and allows you to budget more accurately for increases in staff. Your provider should also make sure that your equipment is kept current.

This type of arrangement is very similar to leasing equipment. It will never really belong to you and you are likely to spend more over the life of the contract than you would have spent if you purchased the equipment outright.

Peer-to-Peer Networking or a Server?

If your business is small, the chances are very good that you are operating with a peer-to-peer network. While you may not have heard that term before, it means pretty much what it says – every computer in the network is a peer to the others. No one is more important 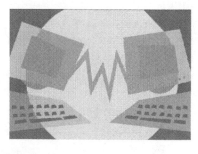 or particularly any different than any of the others. The word peer when we are talking about networks means just about the same thing as it does if we were talking about a peer review or a jury of your peers.

As your business grows, you will get to the point where a peer-to-peer network isn't going to keep up with the increasing demands of your business. If you share files on your network, you will start to run into problems when you have more than 10 computers. Desktop versions of Windows – like XP, Vista and Windows 7 – limit the number of connections that can be made from other desktops. Windows XP only allows 10 connections to be made to a single system. In Vista and Windows 7, the limit has been raised to 20.

If you exceed the connection, you will suddenly find that some people are not able to access the information they need simply because they are the last one to try to connect to the system that contains the data. Even before the limit is reached, the employee using that system may notice that the system is not responding as well as it should.

The hard limitations of desktop operating systems are not the only reasons to look at installing a server for your business. A server environment can provide features and functionality that are not available in a peer-to-peer network. You may be able to benefit from a server before you start to have problems with your peer-to-peer setup.

We recently installed a server for The Stark Agency, an independent insurance agency operating in the Lansing area for over

36 years. When asked about the problems that were starting to surface with the peer-to-peer network and the decision to implement a server, owner Gary Stark said, "We had grown beyond our current peer-to-peer network and were in need of a true server based network. This was deemed necessary to protect the information that we keep about our clients as well as providing the reliability that was now somewhat lacking due to exceeding our current hardware. Our client's security is always first and foremost in our minds, so safeguarding that requires us to take all prudent measures to keep prying eyes out."

If you have a business with 5 or more employees in the office, there are some very compelling reasons you might want to consider upgrading to Microsoft's Small Business Server.

Instant Remote Access, From Home or On the Road

Want to work from home as if you are sitting in the office? A server can enable you to do this. Some companies are actually allowing employees to work remotely to save on office space. It's not uncommon to find companies getting rid of their expensive office space to create a virtual office where all of their employees work from home. This saves a tremendous amount of money on rent and expenses, and studies show that employees are happier and more productive to boot.

You can find more information about working remotely in the chapter on Telecommuting and Remote Access.

Tighter Security Against Hackers and Viruses

Having a server provides a central point of access that can be defended against hackers and viruses. Since all the PCs on the network connect through that central portal, it's easier to keep anti-virus updates current and security systems in place. You'll also be able to manage and monitor employees' Internet access, block spammers, and automatically remove dangerous email attachments to help prevent virus attacks.

More Complete and Reliable Backups

A server will consolidate all the data residing on your desktops and enable you to back everything up at once. Often companies have over half of their critical data and documents residing on individual PCs. If one of those PCs gets compromised, corrupt or experiences a major hardware failure, you could easily lose all of that data!

Virtualization

One of the technologies that is receiving a great deal of press these days is virtualization. Virtualization is a technology that allows one physical box to run multiple operating systems simultaneously. Advances in technology make it possible for many virtual machines to be hosted on one physical machine while still providing plenty of power for the virtual machines.

Server Virtualization

Server virtualization is allowing data centers to pack more processing power into fewer square feet. This means lower power requirements for each server and ultimately lowers the cost of using servers located in data centers.

At the extreme end, a single physical box with the fastest processors available and maximum memory can run as many as 15 virtual servers. Large corporations would configure several servers, each with a specific function. A large data center can utilize this technique to get the maximum number of servers into the minimum amount of space while reducing power requirements and generate significantly more revenue per square foot.

While I have just described a very expensive machine, it is far less expensive than 10 or 15 separate servers. Just as important as the upfront cost, this configuration generates less heat and requires less energy and physical space than 10 or 15 physical servers. At the last Intel technical training I attended, I learned that if I have 184 four year old servers, I can replace them with 21 new servers and see a return on my investment in 8 months. For a growing data center, that is certainly significant!

But most of us don't have 184 servers and many of us have only one. Sometimes though, a software vendor providing a line of business application may state that their application needs to run on a dedicated server. You may also have employees who work remotely using terminal services, newly renamed as remote desktop services. It is advisable to set up a separate server to provide that functionality and not allow your employees to login to your main server directly. Suddenly, you may need several servers to provide the security and functionality that you need. Of course, you may also want to consider using some of these applications in the cloud (more on exactly what that means in the next chapter on cloud computing), but let's just assume that you want to keep everything in house.

Certainly, you can purchase multiple servers, but you should also consider buying a physical server that is powerful enough to run 3 or 4 virtual servers. This allows you to realize all of the benefits of having separate servers – remote capabilities and a line of business application isolated on separate servers, email and user control on a third, and general file sharing services on a fourth. If you have an existing server, you can purchase the new physical server and implement the virtual servers one at a time.

When comparing this solution to purchasing just a single new server to run your new line of business application, you will spend more money, but will likely see a number of side benefits, depending on the age of the server you are replacing. Your new server will likely generate less heat and require less power than your old server, and certainly less than having two servers. Less space will be required for the single server.

Depending on the age and capabilities of the server you are replacing and the exact specifications of the new system, you are also likely to notice an improvement in performance. And if the system is not performing exactly the way you expect, it is easy to reallocate memory to achieve maximum performance. And if your needs change and even more memory is needed, it is simply added to the physical box and then allocated to the machines that need more memory!

Desktop Virtualization

An idea that is becoming increasingly popular is the use of virtual desktops. The concept is similar to that of virtual servers, except that the end user needs some type of device to access the virtual desktop, which is hosted by a server. The device could be a conventional desktop PC, laptop, smartphone or thin client. The server may be housed in your office, or it may be a remote server. You may see or hear the acronym VDI for Virtual Desktop Infrastructure when desktop virtualization is being discussed.

While the user's device is used to log in to the virtual desktop, all of the processing is actually occurring on the server that is hosting the virtual desktops. This type of arrangement is very attractive in environments where you do not want users to have control over their desktops. It is also convenient when all users need to access the same application and if users are moving from desktop to desktop. For example, many medical offices, where doctors and nurses are moving from exam room to exam room, are using thin clients and virtual desktops.

There are several advantages to using virtual desktops. These advantages include:

- Provisioning new desktops is much simpler, and therefore less expensive
- Reduced downtime in the event of client hardware failure
- Lower costs to deploy new applications
- Longer refresh cycles for client desktops
- Increased stability of desktop environments due to limitations generally placed on individual users
- Thin clients require less energy and maintenance than traditional PCs

But virtual desktops may not be the answer for every environment and may pose potential security risks if the network is not properly managed. Additional limitations include:

- Loss of user autonomy and privacy
- Challenges when setting up printers and other peripherals
- Difficulties with complex applications, such as multimedia
- Higher initial deployment costs of virtual environment

Cloud Computing

If you follow technology news, you have no doubt heard or read something about cloud computing. Of course, the article probably assumed that you were already familiar with the term and may have left you wondering what cloud computing is all about.

When someone talks about 'the cloud', you can simply replace "cloud" with "internet". Although not everyone in the industry agrees on a definition of cloud computing, I'm going to define it as using a network of resources that are located on the Internet, and which may or may not be shared by others.

Perhaps the best way to explain this is to think back about 15 or 20 years to early personal computers. If you wanted to be able to get directions and print maps to the places you were going, you had to purchase software and a database to be able to do it. Microsoft Streets and Trips was one such application. Today, maps are available online from Google, MapQuest, Yahoo! and Bing. Not only can you see a map of where you are going and get directions, you can look at satellite and street views, and search the surrounding area for restaurants, hotels, shopping or anything else you might want! And in this example, there isn't any charge to the end user for the service.

There are many more recent examples of business applications that are available in the cloud. Salesforce.com offers sales and CRM software as cloud based solutions. You can't buy their software, you can only subscribe to it. Google offers cloud applications ranging from Gmail to video sharing. Google promises to save you money and reduce IT hassles when you switch from Microsoft applications to Google's hosted versions. This type of solution is often called Software as a Service or SaaS. You may also hear this type of shared arrangement referred to as a public cloud.

Another way to approach cloud computing is to purchase a server, but locate it in a data center rather than in your office. You can also rent servers in the data center for a monthly fee. Either way, you can access the resources from anywhere there is an Internet connection, but now you have more control over the environment. You likely can implement a backup solution that makes you comfortable and you know that you are the only organization using these same resources. In this scenario, you have control of who accesses your resources and how the connection is made. This scenario is a private cloud – it is only accessible to those that you allow to access it.

If you rent a server, you should be able to arrange for monthly rental of the licenses you need for accessing the server and for applications as well. The advantage of this approach is that the number of licenses can be increased and decreased on demand. Some companies also offer the ability to increase or decrease the capabilities of the rented server on demand. This is possible because of the virtualization technology discussed in the previous chapter. If you need more disk storage or more memory, it is easily allocated to you. Likewise, if you need less, it can be deallocated and your monthly expense is reduced. Some companies even offer hourly billing so your monthly rate is increased or decreased immediately. These on demand scaling capabilities are sometimes referred to as utility computing. Like electricity, you pay only for what you use.

So What are the Advantages of Cloud Computing?

There are so many ways to think about cloud computing that it is a bit difficult to summarize the advantages and disadvantages into a neat little package. In the public cloud example, all of the servers belong to someone else and are accessible through the Internet. All you need is a workstation and a fast, reliable Internet connection anywhere in the world and you have access. You completely eliminate the need to purchase and maintain a costly server, swapping that cost for monthly or annual fees for the services you need.

Other advantages include:

1. Eliminates unplanned down time due to power outages, Internet service interruptions and human error at the server location. Of course, your home or office can still suffer from any of those issues.
2. Enables you and your employees to work from home or on the road just as if you were sitting at your desk in the office.
3. If you use a virtual server, virtualization eliminates the capital expenditure for equipment and replaces it with a monthly operating expense. This should reduce your taxes, but you should consult with your CPA to determine the tax savings in your situation. If you are just starting out, it can also free up resources for activities that lead directly to revenue generation.
4. Technology – both hardware and software – is automatically updated and upgraded without additional expense. Of course, if you are using hosted applications, like Salesforce.com, you may not have any control over when the software is upgraded. This can force you to adapt to changes and new features at times that are inconvenient for you.
5. For SaaS solutions, you aren't locked into a product you don't like. If you find that you aren't getting what you expected from the solution, it is easy to try another one because you haven't made an expensive software purchase.
6. Allows you to take advantage of technologies that are otherwise unaffordable. Some software has been designed and written for very large companies, making the solution very expensive to purchase outright. SaaS makes the solution available to small companies and levels the playing field. The same is true of hardware. You may not be able to afford the latest technology, but you can afford a slice of it located in someone else's data center.
7. Reduces space and energy requirements in your office.

Some industry analysts are predicting that one day we will do everything in the cloud and no one will have their own server. Perhaps, but for now, there continues to be a mix of companies who want to move everything to the cloud, while others move nothing to the cloud (with the exception of free services like mapping) and others who settle on a blended solution, moving certain applications to the cloud while keeping others local.

What Should I Look For When Moving to the Cloud?

The single most important factor to consider is the reliability of the vendor or vendors you are considering working with. You are considering putting your business records and processes in the hands of a third party and you want to be sure that the vendor has a proven track record.

Choose carefully. If the vendor you choose suddenly goes out of business, you may find that your business is unable to operate.

Telecommuting and Remote Access

Telecommuting is a fast growing trend among small and medium businesses that is drastically increasing productivity, cutting costs, and driving more profit to the bottom line.
Simply stated, telecommuting is nothing more than allowing your staff to work from home or while on the road.

Sure it doesn't sound very exciting when you first hear it, but when you see the bottom line impact it can have on profits and productivity and talk to business owners who rave about how much money it's saving them, you'll start to see what all the excitement is about. While this is not a new concept, recent advancements in remote access technology and security have made it very affordable and easy for even micro business owners.

Why would a business want to do this? Some businesses are being forced to because they've run out of office space or to accommodate "road warriors." But many are doing it for these reasons…

- Business owners (and key managers) working 60+ hours a week are using it as a way to continue working after hours and on weekends from the convenience of their home office.
- Allowing employees to work from home means businesses can cut back on office space, lowering rent and utility bills – and according to a recent survey of small businesses, nearly 40% of small and medium businesses have (or plan to) cut down office space and allow employees to work remotely from home to save money. Not only is this lowering overhead, but it's making for happier employees who no longer have to fill their gas tanks.
- Telecommuting actually increases employee productivity, lowers stress levels, and improves retention. Contrary to what

33

you may believe, employees who work from home tend to work more, not less. Because the computer is right there in their home, they will often put in extra hours during the evening and on weekends when they normally wouldn't be able to access the network. Plus, employees working on detailed programs, graphics, and projects tend to get more done when they don't have to deal with office distractions.

- Some companies are allowing their employees to work from home two or three days out of a week instead of giving them a raise – a bonus many will gladly take over more money. This also works well if you have limited office space because employees can rotate desk usage.

- It allows you to keep great employees that need or want to relocate, need to stay home to take care of a sick family member, or who are sick, injured, pregnant, or otherwise unable to physically come into the office.

One of the biggest fears many business owners have about allowing people to work from home is the loss of control they have over that person. They believe that without someone standing over them, employees will goof off during work hours and become LESS productive.

But the hard results prove something very different…

Telecommuting has grown at a steady 3% per year for more than 15 years. Currently, more than 23 million people are working from home at least one day a week. The increase in teleworking programs is no accident – it really IS working.

Admittedly, original telecommuting experiments were "do-gooder" projects focused on being earth friendly and generating business savings by reducing use of high priced big city office space. However, when businesses started seeing how it drastically improved turnover and productivity, this "fad" became a hot trend.

Take the Los Angles Bank for example; they decided to test telecommuting to see if it would help their 33% turnover rate. Here were the results…

The experiment worked and within a year the turnover rate was cut to nearly zero and to everyone's surprise productivity went up 18% saving the regional bank more than $3 million dollars per year.

Since then there have been numerous, well documented program studies reflecting promising results. For instance, AT&T allowed employees to telecommute on a regular basis from home in a New Jersey office of 600 people.

Over a 5 year period a region of AT&T saved more than $11 million annually. Half the savings came from real estate savings while the other came from a measured increase in incremental work hours from employees who were able to have a higher level of concentration with fewer interruptions.

You're probably thinking, "But I don't have 600 employees…how does this apply to me?" No matter how small your business or your real estate situation, you can save money. It'll just be a bit smaller than AT&T, but…

On average, small businesses report saving $85,000 to $93,000 per year in lower turnover, reduced operating costs (gas, utilities, and office space) and increased productivity after implementing teleworking programs. (Source: International Teleworking Advocacy Group)

Of course, telecommuting might not be right for every employee on staff, but it is a great option (and reward) for key managers or employees who are self-motivated and measured by results rather than hours worked.

We recently implemented a remote access solution for Cardinal Fabricating in Williamston, Michigan. When we talked to Charlene Bodary, Purchasing and Inventory Control Manager, after the implementation, she talked about how much she appreciates being able to work from home. "Being able to remote into the office network makes it easy to stay on top of things that need to be done at work. I can go home at the end of the day and still take care of things that didn't get done during the work day."

How Do I Get Started?

Before you go "whole hog" with telecommuting and remote access, we recommend conducting a small test where you (and possibly a few key managers) are set up to work from home.

Once you are comfortable with the concept, you may start allowing a few key employees to work from home one day a week or a couple of days a month. Or, you can simply allow employees to use it while traveling or if they are forced to stay home to take care of a child, on a snow day, etc.

But the single most important thing for you to do first is find a very experienced IT consultant who will recommend and implement the right technology to support YOUR specific situation and needs. This is unbelievably important to avoiding expensive mistakes and unnecessary frustration.

There is no "one size fits all" solution; the best solution is greatly dependent on your specific business needs, the applications you use, how many people will be accessing your systems remotely, the available equipment and dozens of other factors. That's why you want to look for a consultant who meets the following criteria:

1. **Look for a consultant who has experience setting up remote access and STRONG (and recent) client references**. Do you really want to be the person who "pays" for your consultant's training? I've found that the price to correct problems created by novices is much greater than the cost to do it right the first

time with an experienced technician. Ask for recent references and call them! Past performance is generally a good gauge of future performance.

2. **Make sure they do a THOROUGH evaluation up front.** If your consultant doesn't insist on doing a thorough evaluation BEFORE handing you a proposal, do NOT hire them! If they don't do their homework they could easily sell you the wrong solution, causing you to have to spend MORE money, MORE time, and have MORE frustration getting to what you really need. Most consultants will do a quick, cursory review and provide a free recommendation (proposal) because they want to close the deal fast. Here is a short list of the things they should investigate or ask you:

   - What are your overall goals and specific objectives for allowing your employees to work from home or on the road?
   - How many employees will be working remotely? Will they be accessing the network at the same time or at different times?
   - What applications (including specialty or proprietary applications) and data will your employees need to access?
   - What type of devices will your staff use to access the network? (Home computers, PDAs, Blackberries, laptops, etc.)
   - What type of Internet connection will be available on the sending AND receiving end?
   - What levels of security do you want in place?
   - What level of monitoring do you want in place? For example, are there certain web sites and content you want "off limits?"
   - Will the remote worker need to print documents?
   - What are your 1 year and 3 year plans for growth?

3. **Make sure they are able to TRAIN you and your staff.** So many computer consultants are great at installing the "stuff" but fall short on training you and your staff how to use the

great "whiz-bang" technology they've just sold you. Make sure you hire someone who is able and willing to do the "hand holding" required when installing any new process or technology…we're only human after all.

4. **Make sure they can provide help desk support AFTER hours.** One of the main appeals to teleworking is the ability to work at night or on weekends; that means you need someone to be "on-call" during those off-peak hours if you or your employees have technical problems logging in or accessing the network. Bottom line – if your consultant doesn't offer after-hours support, don't hire them to do the job. There is no benefit to having remote access if you have to wait until Monday or 9am the next day for support.

5. **Make sure they INSIST on maintaining the network.** Virtual office networks require more "care and feeding" to make sure they work properly and stay secure. You cannot "set it and forget it" or you're asking for problems. Only hire someone who is prepared to perform regular check-ups and updates of your network, usually under a maintenance or managed services plan.

6. **Look for someone who can help you understand and solve the phone piece of the puzzle, not just the network access piece.** If you want your work-from-home employee to be able to make and receive calls and APPEAR as though they are in the office to the caller, then look for someone who can set up your phone system to work with your remote employee's home phone or cell phone. Usually this can be accomplished with VoIP technology (Voice Over Internet Protocol). Confirm that whoever you hire can either provide these services or has a partnership with a reputable vendor who has this expertise. You can find more information about selecting a phone system in the chapter titled Phone Systems.

7. **Make sure your consultant is willing and able to be a vendor liaison for your specific business applications or other specialty applications.** It's amazing how many critical applications work fine within the office network, but then slow

down or shutdown when accessed through a remote location. It's important to insure your consultant is able and willing to confirm your applications will operate efficiently remotely, which means they may need to get on the phone with the help desk of one or more of your software vendors. Some consultants do NOT offer this service, or will charge you extra for it.

8. **Look for a consultant who has expertise in setting up employee monitoring and content filtering.** It's more difficult (but not impossible) to protect company secrets and proprietary information when it's stored on a location outside of your office. Therefore, make sure the company you hire has expertise in setting up and managing content filtering and security for remote machines.

Implementing the Right Backup Solution

Have you ever lost an hour's worth of work on your computer? Now imagine if you lost days or weeks of work – or imagine losing your client database, finance records and all of the work files your company has ever produced or compiled.

Or, what if a major storm, flood, or fire destroyed your office and all of your files? Or if a virus wiped out your server...do you have an emergency recovery plan in place that you feel confident in? How quickly do you think you could recover, if at all?

If you do not have good answers to the questions above or a rock-solid disaster recovery plan in place, you are quite literally playing Russian roulette with your business. With the number of threats constantly growing, it's not a matter of if you will have a problem, but rather a matter of when.

That's why every business – large and small – must have a disaster recovery plan in place. But a big mistake many business owners make is thinking that having a tape backup of their data is enough. Let me tell you why that's dangerous thinking...

Tape backups have a failure rate of 100%. Incredible, isn't it? Most people don't realize that ALL tape drives fail at some point. But what's really dangerous is that most companies won't realize it happened until it's too late.

That's what happened to Dr. Paul Flynn, a Lansing area oral and maxillofacial surgeon, who first started working with us in 2005, when he was experiencing problems with his server. He had been told by another vendor that since his server had 3 hard drives, it was virtually guaranteed that there would be no data loss. But just in case, he also had a tape backup system in place. When the server failed, he found that contrary to what he had been told, there was data loss and to make matters worse, the tape backup had not been functioning properly for 3 months.

We were able to get the server running again and restored the data from the most recent backup. Dr. Flynn's staff worked diligently to recreate the information that they could, but some information was irretrievable. Since it was not precisely known who owed Dr. Flynn money for services performed during the time preceding the crash, it is certain that some money was not collected. The exact cost of this incident is impossible to determine, but it was most certainly a five-figure number.

So it's not hard to imagine that thousands of businesses lose millions of dollars worth of data to disasters like fires, power outages, theft, equipment failure, and even simple human error every year. In almost every case, these businesses had some type of tape backup system in place, but were horrified to find out it wasn't working when they needed it most.

While it's impossible to plan for every potential computer disaster or emergency, there are a few easy and inexpensive measures you can put into place that will help you avoid the vast majority of computer disasters you could experience.

1. **Make sure you are backing up your system.** It just amazes me how many businesses never back up their computer network. Once it's gone, it's gone permanently!
2. **Perform a complete data restore to make sure your backups are working properly.** Many business owners set up some type of backup system, but then never check to make sure it's working properly. The WORST time to "test" your backup is after a disaster has happened and you desperately need it!
3. **Keep an offsite copy of your backups.** What happens if a fire or flood destroys your server AND the backup tapes or drive? What happens if your office gets robbed and they take EVERYTHING? Having an offsite backup is simply a smart way to make sure you have multiple, redundant copies of your data!

If you really want to be certain you could recover from a network disaster, you need a disaster recovery plan that fits your particular situation and budget so you can sleep easier at night. The good news is that a little prevention goes a LONG way – but you have to be prepared or you could end up losing big.

Just a Backup, or a Business Continuity Plan?

Many business owners think that if they have a backup procedure, they have it covered. Nothing could be farther from the truth. If you aren't thinking about disaster recovery and business continuity, you may not be prepared when disaster strikes.

Your plan doesn't have to be complicated, time consuming or expensive. Start by asking yourself the following questions...

1. Do you back up your company's data daily to both an onsite and offsite location?
2. Are you absolutely certain that your backup copy is valid, complete and not corrupt? How do you know for sure?
3. If disaster strikes, how would you get your data back, and what would you do during that period of time?
4. Do you have copies of all the software licenses and discs in a safe location that could be accessed in the event of having to rebuild your server?
5. Would you and your employees have a way to access your network remotely if you couldn't get to the office?
6. Do you store important passwords in a secure place that company officers can access if you are unavailable?
7. Do you have a UPS (uninterruptible power supply) device in place to keep your network and other critical data operations running during a power outage?
8. If your phones are down, where will you forward your business calls so you don't lose that business?

9. If a more common "disaster" occurs, such as server hardware failure, do you have equipment onsite to get back up and running the same day?

This is NOT a complete list, but it is a good start to get you thinking in the right direction.

How Do I Know If My Backup Is Good Enough?

To begin with, you will need to determine your tolerance for both data loss and downtime. Only when you have answered those key questions can you evaluate your backup solution to determine if it will meet your needs. You also need to understand that if you determine that you do not want to be down for more than 2 hours and you don't want to lose more than 15 minutes of data, your backup solution will be more expensive than if you determine that you can afford 2 days of downtime and loss of a week's worth of data.

Some of the questions you need to ask as you make that determination include:

- How much revenue (gross and net) does your company generate daily?
- How many employees do you have and what is their cost? What will it be costing you to pay them while you are waiting for your system to be repaired?
- How much of the revenue generated and the work done by your employees is facilitated by or dependent on your IT infrastructure?
- How will a failure be perceived by your customers and your employees – even if it is short lived?
- How quickly can you recover lost files?
- If a server fails, how long will it be before you are back up and running – and what is the opportunity cost of this downtime?

When you evaluate your backup solution, it should compare favorably against this list of desired features:

- Backups should not rely on human intervention.

- ALL files and programs should be backed up.
- Backups should be automated and easy.
- Files should be backed up throughout the day, eliminating the problems caused when a file is modified and then deleted which can mean going back to last night's copy of the file.
- Backups should have no impact on day to day operations.
- Restores should be fast.
- Ability to restore the system to dissimilar hardware in the event of a catastrophe.

When evaluating the offsite portion of your backup solution, there is a separate list of questions to be considered.

- Is the data transfer secure?
- Is the data storage secure?
- What happens if my office is destroyed? Will I be able to receive my data from the offsite location overnight?
- How will I send my initial backup? (Large backups can take days to transmit via the internet.)
- Is the offsite location geographically separate from my location, providing additional protection from disaster?
- How much will the offsite storage cost?
- Is the offsite solution compliant with relevant regulations – PCI, HIPAA, SEC, SOX or GLBA?

What Should I Expect From My Backup Solution?

Remember that your expectations need to be guided by your tolerance for downtime and data loss, but assuming that you have a limited tolerance for both, here are the key features that you should expect.

1. **Backups should be near real time** – as frequently as once every 15 minutes.
2. **You should have a complete image backup**. This means that your entire server is backed up, including open files.
3. **Restores should be intuitive, flexible and fast**.

4. **Secure offsite transfers that don't interfere with work**. You should expect that offsite transfers will not use all of the available bandwidth during working hours to allow normal work to continue completely unaffected. You also need to know that the data is completely encrypted so that if it is intercepted, it cannot be stolen.
5. **Secure remote storage** – The offsite storage location should be secure and data should be stored encrypted to be absolutely sure that there is no unauthorized access to data.
6. **Monitored and verified** – Make sure that the company providing the service is monitoring and verifying the backup 24 x 7. They should also be performing periodic test restores to be absolutely certain that the data will be available when you need it.
7. **Virtualization** – In the event that your server fails, you want a solution that can virtualize – or pinch hit – for your server while you are waiting for repairs to be made. Virtualization capabilities should also be tested on a regular basis to make sure that everything will go smoothly in the event of a disaster.

Tell Me More About Virtualization

Suppose for a moment that your server has crashed. You place a service call with the hardware manufacturer and find out that your contract only provides for service during business hours and since it is already 3pm, no one will be onsite before 8am tomorrow. You are working on a proposal that has to be delivered by 10am so this is horrible news.

If your backup solution is capable of virtualization, your IT provider can simply perform the necessary steps to create a virtual server on the backup device and boot it. All of your workstations can now connect to the virtual server and access all of the data just as if your server was still operating. Since the system has been configured to backup every 15 minutes, there is little data loss and no reconfiguration necessary to continue working.

45

While you are operating on the virtual server, the system continues to backup every 15 minutes AND send data offsite to continue protecting you from more serious disasters. Depending on the volume of data on your server, this virtualization process takes less than an hour and you are able to complete your proposal and deliver it on time to your prospect.

Remember the story that I told you earlier in this chapter about Dr. Flynn's crash of 2005? Well, Dr. Flynn recognizes that technology is always changing, and he had been researching various alternatives to the backup solution that was implemented in 2005. So when we introduced our automated backup solution that meets all of the criteria outlined in this chapter – including the ability to send his data offsite through the internet nightly AND provide the ability to virtualize his server in the event of a failure – he signed up immediately. Because data is stored in two offsite locations as well as on the local backup device, Dr. Flynn knows there will be no repeat of the crash of '05!

Phone Systems

Today the lines between various types of technology have blurred to the point where it is hard to tell where your computer network ends and your phone system begins.

In fact, many technology companies provide network support and install phone systems. While there may be companies that can do both of these things well, my experience is that these companies fall into one of two categories. Either they started with phone systems and then started doing network support because it seemed sort of related and they thought they could handle it as well, or they started doing network support and as phone systems evolved and began to interface with the rest of the network, they decided they ought to get into the phone system business as well.

Now, a big company can likely do both things well; but a smaller company is probably going to be stretched too thin. Consequently, they will end up either doing only one thing well, or they won't do either thing well. A small company is going to be much more focused in the area where their roots are, and may well give higher priority to the clients in their traditional market.

It's really not necessary that you get your phone system from the same company that provides on going network support. But it is important that your network support company have a good working relationship with your phone system company. If you have signed up for a support plan that includes vendor management, then you certainly have every right to expect that your network support company will help you select the right phone system and vendor and will work through the integration issues with them at the time of installation.

Next to your server and workstations, your phone system is one of the most significant investments that you will make for your company. It can be even more expensive and frustrating than necessary if you make any of the costly mistakes that trap buyers into:

- Paying too much for unnecessary bells, whistles and ongoing maintenance.
- Getting locked into a complicated system that can't be supported in house or expanded without significant upgrade costs.
- Getting locked into an expensive and limiting contract.
- Not getting the features you need in the base package and subsequently having to pay a LOT more for "upgrades" and add-on services that you thought were included.
- Not sizing the system properly for current and future growth needs.

Unfortunately, a lot of companies are sold an overpriced, complicated phone system simply because they didn't know all of the options available to them, or simply because they didn't know how to ask the right questions when interviewing phone vendors.

With so many choices, it can be very difficult to make an educated decision without spending days or weeks researching all of the vendors and options you have. Use the points below as a quick reference to help you make the absolute best decision when buying a new phone system.

1. **Make sure you plan for future needs.** Before you buy a system, make sure you have answers to the following questions to plan ahead for future needs:
   - How many new employees do you think you will hire over the next 5 years?
   - Will you have remote offices or employees working from home?
   - Do you think you will open other branches in the future?

- How many phone lines will you need? Don't forget to take into account lines you may need for conference calls or for features like "follow me dialing".
- Do you need the ability to do call reporting / call accounting?
- What training tools are available for the proposed system, and what is their cost?

Look for a system that will allow you to add new features and expand your system later on at virtually no additional cost. A good question to ask your vendor is, "If we decide to add these features later on, what will it cost us in total hardware, software, training and services?"

2. **Make sure you purchase an "open" system.** A truly open system is one that will work with the equipment you already own or plan to purchase later on including phone headsets, toll fraud equipment, or tabletop conferencing equipment. Otherwise, you'll be locked into buying that vendor's equipment only, forcing you to pay top-dollar or have limited options. How do you know if the system you are buying is truly an open system? Make sure it:

- Works with off-the-shelf, standard telephones.
- Runs on an industry standard operating system (such as Asterisk or Microsoft Windows).
- Includes SIP (Session Initiation Protocol) capabilities for working with emerging technologies and flexibility with other SIP systems.
- Can easily be maintained in-house (change extensions, add or delete users, change features) by end-users with a graphical user interface software and browser based views and tools.

- Can interface seamlessly with off-the-shelf software applications such as customer management and sales force automation without the need for complex programming.
- Will work with any other "open" phone equipment you purchase.

3. **Make sure you have plenty of space for voice mail.** Don't underestimate the value of voice mail. The last thing you want a customer to hear is, "Sorry, you cannot leave a voice mail message because this user's box is full." To avoid this all together, make sure your system has unlimited ports of voice mail. Also, your system should have the ability to set up an unlimited number of voice mailboxes.

4. **Make sure that the system can be maintained in-house.** Anyone who has ever owned a traditional PBX or legacy telephone system knows the incredible costs for maintenance, support, and upgrades. In fact, because all maintenance activities on these types of phone systems requires vendor involvement at $150 or more per visit, **lifetime maintenance costs on a legacy PBX typically run as high as 40% of the system cost**.

   In other words, that $50,000 phone system will really cost you $70,000 before you're done. If you want to add, delete, or change a user's extension, can you do it in house or do you need to call the vendor, wait 2 days for the guy to come out, and pay $150? This is a no-brainer; make sure your system can easily be supported in-house by end-users and you'll save a lot of time and money.

5. **Make sure technical support is included in the installation.** With any new system, you are bound to run into a few snags and have questions. Make sure the vendor provides free, unlimited phone and e-mail support for at least 30 days after installation. You should also see how easy it is to move,

change, or otherwise alter the extensions, voice mail boxes, and other features of your system. After the initial included support period, make sure the cost for ongoing support is reasonable, and that you understand what level of support will be covered by the fee.

6. **Make sure you are buying a system that has "next generation" features already embedded.** While you might not think you want or need next generation features such as Voice Over IP or VoIP (the ability to run voice calls over the Internet to save on usage costs), web interactions, and e-mail integration, the system you buy should allow you to implement these features very inexpensively sometime in the future.

   Look for a system that embeds:
   - Voicemail
   - Messaging
   - Automatic call distribution
   - Operator console
   - Call forwarding
   - Call detail reporting
   - Follow-me dialing
   - Web based click-to-talk

   Many new systems will embed these features into an effectively priced offering, eliminating the need to purchase these applications separately down the road. If the system you are considering requires complex infrastructures, implementations, or pricing schemes to add these features on, look for another system.

Document Management Systems

If a gust of wind suddenly came through your office, would it leave you with piles of paper chaos? If you still have manual and paper processes, it probably would. It might be your manual service tickets, your 3-ply invoices, or the mountain of paperwork that arrives on your desk from clients that you have to sift through, sort, and file every day. If you're honest, you probably don't have to think too hard to find at least one process in your company that is a giant frustrating paper trail, far from the well-oiled machine you'd like it to be.

If you can't stand the thought of this kind of chaos, you may want to consider document management. Simply put, a document management system is software and hardware installed on your network that can streamline business processes and drastically reduce the amount of paper you use. A document management system saves you money, helps your business run more smoothly, and gives you a sense of pride that everything is running as efficiently as it should be.

Most document management systems also have a document imaging component, which is the term used to describe the way your current paper documents and files become electronic. Typically, your files are scanned in with a multi-function copier/scanner, and the document management software then helps you label and organize that file.

How do you know if a document management system is right for you? Ask yourself the following questions to find out.

1. Do you have at least one employee who files or retrieves documents? Let's say it takes 6 minutes for a $20/hour employee to physically get a file, review what they need, and return it to the file cabinet. If they do this just 3 times a day, it's taking 75 hours and costing you over $1,500 every year. Multiply this by 10 employees and you've got a $15,000 problem. With document management, getting those same files is basically instantaneous, making a big impact on productivity savings.

2. Do you use more than one file cabinet? According to Coopers & Lybrand, the average cost to fill and maintain a single 4-drawer file cabinet is over $6,200 per year (including average cost of floor space). If you've run out of space in your own office and now rent storage space elsewhere, your costs are even higher. Document management eliminates the need for these.

3. In your industry, are there any regulatory compliance issues in regards to storing client information? The medical field has HIPPA, the financial world has Sarbanes-Oxley, and other professionals such as attorneys have an ethical obligation to protect private information. Many other business types have to be compliant with other regulations like the Patriot Act in terms of securing their information. Because of the encryption included, document management provides the security needed to comply with almost any of these regulations.

4. If your paper files were stolen, are you worried about the damage it would cause your business? Would those records be gone forever? It's a lot easier for someone to walk into your office and swipe a file than it is for someone to hack into a document management software, de-code the encryption, and do so without being traced. If your documents and files are stored electronically, and you have a proper backup and disaster recovery plan, your information stays safe, no matter what happens.

5. Do you have employees that work remotely or have multiple locations? With the right document management system, files and electronic records of any kind are easily accessible from anywhere. Plus multiple people can view the same file at the same time, something nearly impossible with a physical file.

6. Have you ever spent more than a couple of minutes searching for a document on your server? Probably one of the most frustrating events in any work day is combing through the endless files on your server to search for the document you need. After a few minutes of futile effort to find what you need, your frustration turns to anger and you either turn into a raving lunatic, recruiting others to now join the search party for the blasted file that you KNOW is there, or you give up altogether – neither of which is very good for productivity. Document management ends this problem by giving you an easily searchable, organized place to store your files.

If you answered "yes" to any of the above questions, then a document management system may be just what you're looking for.

Security

Throughout this book, security has been mentioned as it specifically relates to one area or another. If you've never had issues with security, it is easy to dismiss security as something only big companies need to worry about.

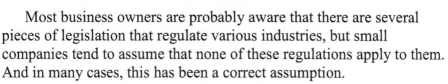

Let me assure you that nothing could be further from the truth. Cybercriminals are always looking for new targets, and if you haven't put any security measures in place, you will be an easy target. You don't have to be a big company to have your email server used as a relay for spam, effectively bringing your own email to a screeching halt.

Most business owners are probably aware that there are several pieces of legislation that regulate various industries, but small companies tend to assume that none of these regulations apply to them. And in many cases, this has been a correct assumption.

However, some states have enacted laws that apply to any organization that touches or retains personal information. In Massachusetts, the law applies if you retain information for a Massachusetts resident, even if you are not a Massachusetts company.

There is also federal legislation pending that could well result in regulations similar to those that have taken effect in Massachusetts and would affect every business in the country.

Even if there is no legal obligation to put security measures in place, you could still be faced with a huge issue if you have sensitive information that is breached. If you have enough information about your customers that someone could assume their identity with it, then you have sensitive information. And if you have employees you certainly have enough information to allow someone else to assume their identities.

Surprisingly, while there are regulations specifying how data should be safeguarded, there is little federal requirement dictating how you should respond if data is compromised. That doesn't mean that you shouldn't worry about your response, and you may want to consult with a firm that handles these types of situations.

If you find yourself in such a situation, there are four key steps you should take.

1. Contain the breach and make a preliminary assessment. This is also when you need to contact law enforcement to make them aware of the situation. This is the time to determine who needs to be involved within your organization and who will need to be notified outside of your organization. This is not the time to notify those people though, and above all, work with law enforcement before making notification.

2. Evaluate the risks involved with the breach. You will need to identify the kinds of data lost and if it is encrypted or not. Look at the cause and the extent of the breach, the individuals affected and assess the foreseeable harm. If the data is encrypted, then there may be little foreseeable harm. You may want to let your employees know what has happened at this stage. You don't want them operating on rumors!

3. Determine who should be notified and when, as well as what should be in the notice. Also consider who will make the notification. It is important that you designate one person to be the spokesperson for your organization so that you are delivering a consistent message. You may want to engage a Public Relations Agency to handle this for you. It is extremely important that you be completely transparent in your disclosure and do not hide any relevant information. The damage caused to your reputation by being any less than completely truthful will likely far outweigh the damage caused by the breach itself. Don't forget to include law enforcement, credit reporting agencies, regulators, insurance carriers, customers and your employees.

4. Lastly, work to prevent future issues. This is the time to review your physical and system security, as well as review your policies and procedures. Address the deficiencies that have been brought to light and use the opportunity to identify other weaknesses.

During the entire process, document every step. If regulators become involved, you will be glad that you have a record of the actions taken at each step of the way.

Acceptable Use Policies

According to an article written by Workforce.com, 31.8% of publicly traded companies in the U.S. were compelled to investigate a suspected violation of privacy or data protection because an employee of the company used the company's electronic media (email, the Internet, instant messaging, etc.) inappropriately.

In a report by Forrester Consulting and Proofpoint, 26% of companies surveyed say they saw their business affected because sensitive or embarrassing information had been leaked this way—and the trend is not slowing down.

The Biggest Problem – Your Employees

Problems included losing trade secrets and client files to slander and defamation lawsuits—and almost 28% of the companies that participated in this survey said they had terminated an employee for misusing email. Blogs and message boards were also cited as being

problematic.

The biggest problem is that electronic media spreads FAST and your employees are the weakest link in the IT security chain. If an employee sends an inappropriate joke from your company email address, it can spread like wildfire causing harm to your company's reputation, not to mention lost business and costly lawsuits.

You can set up a firewall, encryption, anti-virus software, and password protection up to your ears, but it won't save you from the employee who posts his access information to a public web site. Most security breaches, viruses, spyware, and other network problems are a result of human error—an end user unknowingly downloading an infected file, emailing confidential information, or disabling their anti-virus, to name a few.

How to Protect Your Company

First, companies should have an acceptable use policy (AUP) in place that all employees are required to read, understand, and sign. An AUP simply outlines how employees can — and can't — use company email, Internet, or other electronic media. You need to train your employees on what is and what is NOT acceptable behavior.

But that is just the starting point – if the requirements on your AUP are not enforced, employees will accidentally (or intentionally) violate your rules. That's why you should also consider investing in good email and web filtering software.

Just having a policy in place will act as a deterrent for such activities, and if something is going on — like an employee leaking confidential information to a competitor or sending racial or sexist jokes through your company's email —you'll be able to nip it in the bud before it comes back and bites you in the form of a lawsuit.

Tips to Encourage Compliance

If you want your employees to actually adhere to your security policies, here are a few tips -

- **Keep it simple.** A long, confusing policy that looks like a legal document is about as easy to read as the instruction manual for your digital camera. Make the policies clear and easy to read. Give examples and include screen shots where necessary.
- **Provide group training.** Many companies make the mistake of distributing their AUP by email and telling employees they must read it on their own. This gives the employees the option of NOT reading and simply signing and submitting. You don't need hours of classroom training but a simple 15 or 20-minute session will force even the most reluctant users to learn a thing or two.
- **Keep employees updated.** To add to the above tip, make sure you update employees on a regular basis to keep the policies fresh in their minds and to educate them about new threats.

- **Explain the consequences of not following the policy.** This is both explaining the negative effects to the business as well as disciplinary actions that will be taken if they refuse to follow policy. Occasional violators should be warned, and habitual violators should be disciplined.
- **Monitor their behavior.** The best policy in the world won't work if it's not enforced. There are many tools on the market that can do this for you automatically. Courts have ruled that an employer's monitoring of its employees' emails and other computer related activities during work hours and/or on company owned equipment, Internet and email accounts is not illegal.

What to Include

Some common rules that should be included with most AUPs are:

- All sensitive or confidential data must be encrypted before sending across the web. For example, many doctors' offices use instant messaging (IM) to communicate from the front desk to the back office. However, many don't realize that this is a violation of HIPAA because IM is not a secure way to transmit information about a patient or their health conditions.
- A restriction on sharing confidential information about the company, its clients or the people working there. With social media as popular as it is, you don't want an employee writing all about the latest company scandal on their MySpace page; it's just not good for business!
- Prohibition against visiting web sites that contain pornography, racism, sexism, gambling, or email with any such content sent from your business. Remember, even "innocent" jokes with this type of content can leave a huge black mark on your company's reputation.
- Absolutely no downloading of music files or other programs that are not approved by management. "Innocent"

screen saver programs and jokes often contain nasty viruses that could bring down your entire system or invite a hacker into your network.

Your IT company should be able to help you write your AUP. They may even have a sample document that you can use with a few modifications to fit your specific situation. They can also help you train your staff so that everyone understands the risks involved when the policy is not followed.

There are also many tools available that allow you to monitor and/or block network activity. Your IT company will be able to suggest a solution that meets your needs. Be sure that you will receive regular reports showing violations and that you are able to drill down into the detail so that you know who is responsible for the violations.

Password Policies

When you set up your network, you will want to give serious consideration to implementing a password policy. While I have worked with many clients who consider passwords to be an inconvenience and ask us to disable passwords, that is not the action that we recommend. A full server solution will do nothing to enhance security if you systematically disable all of the features designed to keep the system secure.

Password policies are important for several reasons. I have listed just a few here to get you thinking about the risks and problems that can be caused by failing to enforce a password policy.

If you have no passwords, anyone in your office will be able to access the information on your network. Do you trust the cleaning contractor that much?

One of your computers is badly infected with spyware and viruses. When you take it to the repair shop to be cleaned, you are told that someone has been visiting pornographic websites. Since that is a violation of your AUP, you want to discipline or dismiss the person responsible. Unfortunately, you don't know who is responsible because there are no passwords and anyone could have logged into the account.

You discover there are icons on the server's desktop that weren't there the last time you sat down at the network console. None of your employees know anything about them. Suddenly you wonder if someone from outside your organization has accessed your server.

Hopefully, those few examples have convinced you that passwords are important! Each person who logs into your network should have their own unique username and password.

It is very simple to implement some rules for passwords that will be enforced by the server. Once you have set them, make them part of your AUP so employees will know the guidelines and not be surprised when they are asked to change their passwords.

There are five password characteristics that you should consider:

- **Enforce Password History** – This determines the number of new unique passwords a user must set before an old password can be reused. Microsoft recommends a setting of 24. That would mean that you would have to have used 24 different passwords before returning to the original password. You can also turn this feature off, in which case a user could continue using the same password.
- **Maximum Password Age** – This determines how many days a password can be used before the user is required to change it. Microsoft recommends setting this to 42 days, but it can be turned off or set to as many as 999 days.
- **Minimum Password Age** – This determines how frequently a user can change their password. This works in conjunction with password history to prevent a user from changing their password to a new value and then immediately changing it back to its original value. You can turn this feature off or set it to as many as 999 days, but the recommendation is to set it to 2 days. Chances are that the user will have learned their new password by then!
- **Minimum Password Length** – This determines how short passwords may be. Users may be allowed to have blank passwords or you can require that passwords be used. If you use passwords, the minimum length is 4, with 8 the recommended minimum. Passwords can be as long as 28 characters. Short passwords are much easier to guess and are more susceptible to being hacked by automated systems.
- **Passwords Must Meet Complexity Requirements** – This is a setting that is either enabled or disabled. If you enable this feature, passwords will need to follow these rules:
  - Must be at least six characters long
  - Must contain at least three of the following:
    - Uppercase character (A – Z)

63

- Lowercase character (a – z)
- Numeric digit (0 – 9)
- Non-alphanumeric character, such as ! $ * or %
  - Cannot contain three or more consecutive characters from the user name

Enabling this setting forces users to create passwords that are not easily guessed.

So how do you come up with passwords that follow the rules and are easy to remember? One technique involves coming up with a phrase that will be easy for you to remember and substituting special characters for some of the letters. For example, the number 1 can replace a lowercase letter l easily. Similarly, an @ can be used in place of the letter a, and the number 3 for the letter e. So you might start with "angelfoodcake" and then turn that into "Ang3lf00dc@k3". I'll let you decide if that is still the letter l or the number 1!

Online Passwords

Beyond your own internal network, you need to give some serious thought to passwords you use online. To avoid being a victim of cyber criminals, security experts at the University of California, Davis, suggest having two passwords. One would be an easy password that could be used where not much security is needed. The second password would be more intricate and used for banking and other security-sensitive matters. Here are some additional tips to beef up security:

- Never use a proper name or a word that appears in a dictionary of any language.
- Use at least eight characters including upper and lower case, numbers, and symbols. This is much like the complexity requirements just discussed.

- Try using the first letters of words in a quote, phrase, or title. So for example, if your phrase is "a stitch in time saves nine", use "asitsn" as the base for your password, adding numbers or special characters in addition or to replace specific letters.
- Change an element of the password at least quarterly.

Do You HATE Having To Remember Passwords?

If you are like most people, you have a hard time remembering all of the passwords you have to use for various web sites and vendors. Problem is, choosing easy to remember passwords won't thwart the "bad guys." Writing them down is not recommended, and using Microsoft applications to remember your passwords is like walking through a crowd with hundred dollar bills hanging from your pockets.

If you'd like an easy way to not only keep track of all the passwords you use, but also make filling in online forms faster and easier, then I recommend a software product called RoboForm. This inexpensive program completely automates password entering and form filling. The software...

- Memorizes your passwords and logs you in automatically.
- Fills in long registration and checkout forms with one click.
- Encrypts your passwords to achieve complete security.
- Generates random passwords that hackers cannot guess.
- Fights phishing by filling in passwords only on matching web sites.
- Defeats keyloggers by not using the keyboard to type passwords.
- Backs up your passwords and copies them between computers.
- Portable: RoboForm2Go runs from a USB key; no install needed.
- Neutral: works with Internet Explorer, AOL/MSN, Firefox.

Download a free 30 day trial of this software at www.roboform.com/download.html. A word of warning though: if you change your password regularly and are required to enter your old password to create the new one, roboform can create problems. I have a tendency to update it with my new password and then forget them. This makes it extremely difficult to enter the correct password in order to change it.

Email

There is no doubt that email has become an important form of business communication. Most of us rely on email to communicate all types of information. Not only does email replace conventional mail, it has also replaced much of our phone communications.

For many, email communication is not only faster, but also more convenient. Unlike a phone call, the other party does not need to be available when you are ready to communicate. You can send your message off at your convenience, and the recipient can respond when it is convenient. That is much easier than finding a mutually convenient time to talk, and it provides a record of what was said.

How Can I Deal Effectively with the Hundreds of Emails I Receive Daily?

Is email driving you crazy? Every time you delete one, do five more show up? Are you finding it impossible to answer every email you receive? Don't worry, you are not alone!

Some people are even declaring email bankruptcy — they dump every email in their inbox and start over. If that's not an option for you, then here are 10 tips to reduce email overload.

1. **Get a good spam filter.** Even if it saves you just 10 minutes a day, that adds up to over 59 hours a year. Studies have shown that only about 10 percent of email messages are legitimate, so without a good spam filter, expect to delete at least 9 messages for every good message.
2. **Cancel subscriptions to unwanted mailing lists, and opt-out of LEGITIMATE e-zines.** But be careful! Trying to opt-out of spam emails will only alert the sender that they have a LIVE address. Also, make sure you are careful to check the "unsubscribe" or "opt-out" box when purchasing items online.

3. **Ask your friends to remove you from joke groups or chain messages.** Simply explain your situation and, if they are good friends, they'll take you out of their message group.
4. **Don't post or publish your email on web sites.** Spammers will steal it and put it on their lists.
5. **Don't respond to every email you receive.** Yes, it's okay NOT to respond to some emails. If it's a group email, don't respond with "okay" or ":)" — it's not necessary unless the sender is specifically asking you a question or requesting a response.
6. **Be succinct.** Restrict your messages to a few sentences. If you can't, pick up the phone or talk in person. This will avoid the back-and-forth of email conversation.
7. **Take advantage of subject lines.** If possible, put your question in the subject line of your message. If that's not possible, make your subject line very descriptive so the recipient knows what your message is about. Here's another tip; create a set of codes with your coworkers and place them in the subject line to help them process and prioritize messages. For example, use "FYI" for informational messages. Use "AR" for action required and "URG" for urgent messages.
8. **Block time to answer your email and fight the temptation to check your email every few minutes.** You will save yourself a lot of time and be far more productive. When you aren't answering your email, close your email client completely, or at least turn off the audible notification and the pop up messages that let you know new messages have arrived.
9. **Respond to messages when you open them so you only read them once.** If the email requires an action step, schedule the action step and delete it from your inbox.
10. **Set time aside in the morning and the evening to process your inbox.** Shoot for a completely empty inbox. File messages you need to keep and set reminders for messages that require you to follow up.

Are You Contributing to the Problem?

Of course, you also want to be sure that you aren't contributing to the problem. Here are a few tips to keep from adding to the email overload of others…

1. **Be courteous when forwarding an email**. Summarize the thread and why you are sending it at the top of the email.
2. **Don't copy someone on a message unless it is necessary**. And explain why you're copying them. Recipients won't need to guess your intentions. This means fewer back and forth messages.
3. **Use REPLY ALL rarely, if ever**. I'll admit it – this is one of my pet peeves. If one of your friends sends an email to you and several others about something personal, you will likely want to respond with kind and sympathetic words. Be sure you reply only to the sender and not to the entire group. I can't tell you how many times I have received responses from people I don't even know in situations just like this. I've also seen it in response to emails inviting people to an event or to join a group. Unless you think that your decision is likely to affect the decisions of others, you really don't need to share with everyone. On the other hand, if you want the email thread to become a discussion, then by all means, REPLY ALL, but if you find yourself doing this frequently, consider setting up some type of discussion board or forum instead.
4. **Setup Out of Office Replies properly**. When you are out of the office a day or more and will not be responding to email, it is a great idea to set up an out of office reply to let people know when to expect a reply. But do take care to only send the reply once to each person that sends you a message.

What Should I Know About Spam?

You know that spam causes you and your staff to waste untold hours if you aren't able to stop it before it reaches your inbox. But what else do you need to know to make informed decisions about spam and your email.

There are many risks associated with spam, both as a sender and as a receiver. You are no doubt aware that spam can be loaded with viruses and spyware, typically delivered through an attachment and an intriguing subject line. If the subject tells you the message contains a receipt for your new laptop and you don't remember buying one, don't open the attachment. Better yet, be sure you have programs in place to stop messages like these long before they reach your inbox. Then there are the ever present messages classified as phishing spam. These messages attempt to convince you to part with your bank account or credit card information for the purpose of theft or fraud.

But you may not be aware that due to rising email abuse and spam, hundreds of servers at various companies now monitor email accounts to make sure those accounts are not sending out mass emails. If an email account is judged as sending spam, it is put on the "blacklist". Once on the blacklist, your email account is virtually SHUT DOWN because your email is blocked by hundreds or thousands of servers and your message can't be delivered. Big companies who give out email addresses like AOL, Google, and Comcast, for example, will cut off email service to anyone who sends an email to a large number of people at once. Because of this, even if you or your employees innocently send a message to 100 of your clients, you could be without email for days or weeks. So, how do you avoid being "blacklisted"?

1. **Protect Your Server.** Spammers LOVE to find email servers that don't have a proper firewall, anti-virus, and intrusion protection. They get a high from hacking in to these servers and then using them to send out thousands of emails. Plus, with no protection in place, tracking and catching these spammers is nearly impossible. The right protection will also prevent malware from being installed on your server, which can automatically send spam without human interaction.

2. **Don't Allow Employees To Forward Messages.** Unless it is for work related purposes, make a policy that no one is to

forward messages like jokes, photos or videos outside the company. If just four of your employees send out this kind of an email to 30 of their contacts, that's well over 100 people receiving junk mail on the same day from the same email server. This puts you at high risk of being blacklisted.

3. **Have Your Clients and Prospects "Opt-In".** Sometimes companies end up on the blacklist because someone on your list complained and reported your message as spam. If you have your clients and prospects agree via an opt-in form that they want to receive communication from you and confirm their permission, then you'll have better protection against that. Also make sure you keep good records of opt-ins. That way, even if you do get blacklisted, you should be able to get your domain removed from the blacklist quickly.

4. **Make Sure Your Email Is Set-Up Properly.** In addition to protecting yourself from hackers and invasions with software and firewalls, you also need to be sure that your email is configured correctly and is set-up to block outside relays. If you've got the wrong settings in your email account, you could wind up blacklisted, without any email for days or weeks. Incorrectly configured email can also lead to delivery failures to certain recipients, while others are able to receive your email without incident.

5. **Keep Your Email List Up-To-Date.** If someone asks to be removed from your list and you continue to send messages to him, the chances of him reporting your company as a spammer are pretty high. Avoid this by using in-house lists (instead of purchasing one) and contacting your list to verify the information.

What About Sending Email to Clients and Prospects?

Faced with a postal rate increase nearly every year, we're all looking for cost effective ways to reach new customers or keep in touch with current ones.

In the 80's fax blasts were the alternative to costly snail mail. Unfortunately, many firms abused customers' fax machines and Congress enacted severe restrictions and stiff fines virtually shutting down the fax as a marketing tool overnight.

Today the alternative to snail mail is email. True to form, spammers sending out those unwanted "Male Enhancement", "Lose 20 Pounds in 5 Days", or "How to Make Millions at Home Stuffing Envelopes" junk ads caused Congress to jump back into action. In 2003, Congress enacted the CAN-SPAM Act.

Although the Act specifies rules for message presentation, opt out guidelines, labeling for sexually explicit materials, and penalties of up to $11,000 per violation, the law was clearly not intended to exclude legitimate marketers from using email.

In fact, a solid, well-targeted marketing campaign with a strong message can yield extremely high returns while remaining well within the federal guidelines. The difference between running a marketing program and generating spam ads is the difference between being an "invited guest versus an unwanted pest." Too many businesses fall into the latter category.

To avoid the limitations and ensure compliance with the law, businesses are turning to inexpensive bulk emailing services like Constant Contact or iContact. These services provide:

- Email addressed to the recipient from you – open rates for these messages can be as high as 90% .
- Opt out services – Avoid contacting people that don't appreciate your offering.
- Return services - Escape "dead" addresses clogging your email inbox .
- Database updates – Send messages to current and prospective "Live" clients.
- Up-to-date email procedures – Limit your legal risk .

Whether you strike out on your own with email or use a bulk mailing service, it would be wise to check out the law on the web, craft a solid marketing plan with an attractive offer, and always include a link back to your web site or electronic marketing materials to maximize your ROI.

Does Your Email Address Make You Look Like an Amateur?

In business, image is everything; and if you are a small business, I'm sure you want to do everything possible to portray your competence and professionalism. But there is one thing that may be undermining the professional image you are trying so hard to uphold: your email address.

If you are using a hotmail.com, msn.com, yahoo.com or other "free" email address, it's sending a clear message that you are a small home-based business that is not large enough to have your own web site and domain name; and in this day and age, that's a major red flag. Do you really want to make that kind of impression on clients and prospects?

Having an @companyname.com address instantly gives you more credibility. You appear to be more professional and established compared to competitors who are using free email accounts.

The good news is that getting your own domain name and email account is easy. You can search for available domain names and register yours by going to our website, www.KITechnologyGroup.com, and scrolling down to find the "Register a Domain Name" button. There are many other services that will allow you to search for and purchase available domain names. Domain registrations are less than $30 a year, with discounts for longer registrations.

Once you have a domain, you will be able to create the email addresses that you want to use. Even if you are a one person operation, don't think that you are limited to just one email address. You can set up different addresses for different purposes – one for sales and one for customer service perhaps.

And as long as you have a domain name, consider setting up at least a simple website. It doesn't need to be complicated to get started – just tell people the name of your company, how to contact you and what problems you will be able to solve for them.

What About Saving Email?

This may be an issue you have not given much thought to, but it could become a major issue at some point: saving email communications to employees and clients that contain company policy changes, contract changes, alerts or other critical communications.

So why not just save them in your inbox? Because eventually you'll run out of space; and searching through hundreds of thousands of emails is not always a simple and easy task. Here are 5 BIG reasons why you need an email archiving system:

1. **Compliance.** While the emails and data subject to regulatory statutes varies by industry, ALL emails that contain employee and client records, contract negotiations, company policy changes and employee reviews and reprimands should be stored and achieved for easy retrieval.
2. **Litigation Support.** If you are ever sued, you may be ordered by the court to produce documentation to support your case; such documentation includes emails. Problem is, pulling emails off a tape drive backup can be a massive undertaking. In one such case, USB Bank had to pay an IT firm over $265,000 to pull email communications previously sent.
3. **Free Up Storage Space**. If you've ever had your email stop working because you've exceeded your storage space, you know how frustrating this can be. Archiving eliminates this problem finally and forever.
4. **Improve Workflow Systems And Procedures.** Another upside to email archiving is your ability to search, document and organize information pertaining to servicing customers, delivering a product, sending out an RFP, selecting vendors, etc.

5. **Ease Of Finding Emails.** Let's face it; we've all had the daunting task of trying to find an email sent months ago. An email archiving system would allow you to perform searches of both keywords and attachments to find emails in minutes – even seconds – rather than hours or days.

Fortunately, there are several excellent email archiving solutions available today. Email archiving takes the decisions about what to keep and how long to keep it out of the hands of your staff and allows you to make decisions about what email needs to be kept and for how long. Great systems also make it easy to search for the messages you need and to easily follow an email thread or conversation. The information is typically available either through Outlook or your web browser.

And best of all, email archiving doesn't have to be an expensive proposition. For as little as $30 per email address per year, you can have a consistent email policy in place.

How Do I Choose the Right Website Developer?

To a large extent, the questions you need to ask when hiring a website developer are the same questions you should be asking when you hire your computer support company. You will want to check references, ask for fixed pricing, make sure you understand what is included, get everything in writing and do business with a "one man band" carefully.

While many computer support companies also do website development, it doesn't necessarily follow that just because a company is good at one, they will be good at the other. Even if you are happy with the work the company has done in one area, you will want references from the other area before moving forward with your project.

If your computer support company doesn't do web development, they will probably be able to put you in touch with a company that they recommend. The chances are very good that if you have been happy with their services, you will be happy with the web development company they recommend as well. After all, a strong recommendation puts their reputation on the line as well, and they are not going to recommend someone if they are not confident of their abilities.

If your computer support company does web development as well, be sure to ask if the web development team is separate from the computer network support team, or if the same team is responsible for both areas. You don't want someone else's server crash to delay your website rollout.

Beyond that, there are specific questions that you should ask before you sign that web development contract. These questions don't have hard and fast right answers in general, but it is likely that there is one answer that is right for you and your organization.

1. **How much input will I have in the design of my site?** The site is being designed for you and you may have very definite ideas about how you want it to look. Perhaps you have graphics

that have been used for other media that you want incorporated in your website. If you have seen sites that you like, show those to the web developer to make sure that he will be able to incorporate the elements you like in your site. You should also ask who specifically will be creating the design and layout to makes sure you will be comfortable working with them.

2. **How will the site content be created?** If you already have content created, either specifically for your website or for other media, then this should not be an issue. But if you don't have any content, you need to know if you will be responsible for creating it, or if the web developer has a copy writer who can do that for you. Even if you are not a writer, you need to have a clear idea of the message you want on your website. I do not recommend leaving this important decision to a copy writer. You should also ask about images for the website. Will you be using photographs or stock images? If you don't already have the photographs, who will take them, and will there be additional fees for them?

3. **After the site is launched, how will changes be made?** Many, but not all, web developers have started developing websites using a content management system, frequently referred to as a CMS. The advantage of a site written in this way is that you can make changes to your site whenever you need to – and without any specialized knowledge of web programming. Popular CMS's include Joomla, DotNetNuke and WordPress. In most cases, the actual system used isn't really important. The important point is that if the site does not use a CMS, you will have to rely on the web developer to make changes, which will result in additional charges. Of course, if you don't want to make changes yourself, you may not care if the site is or isn't written using a CMS. In that case, just make sure you understand what changes to your site are likely to cost, and how quickly they can be made when required.

4. **Where will the site be hosted?** All websites need to be hosted on a web server. Typically, web servers are located in data centers that provide high availability and very fast internet

connections. Your web developer probably has a webserver where they host the sites they develop, but they may also allow you to host it elsewhere. If the web developer is hosting the site for you, be sure you know if the hosting package includes email hosting if that is a service you also need. Of course, if you have your own email server, then you will not need email services included.

5. **What website statistics will be available and what information will you be given to help you understand them?** Once your website is launched, you will want to know whether or not anyone is visiting it, which pages they view, how they are finding your site and various other bits of interesting data. This is information you should use to improve your site and work on converting site visitors to customers or clients. Your web developer may have their own reports that you can view and analyze, or they may suggest that you use Google Analytics. Google Analytics is a free tool that is simply turned on in your site. Google Analytics are very good and are widely used to analyze web site performance. If your web developer recommends something else, ask why. This may be an attempt to tie you to their web hosting services.

6. **What about search engine optimization (SEO)?** SEO is the use of various techniques to improve your site's ranking by search engines such as Google, Bing and Yahoo. Obviously showing up on the first page of results when your prospects search for a company like yours is a big advantage. Top ranking takes some work and focus on titles, tags, descriptions, keywords and inbound links. Of course before you even consider any of that, you need to have an understanding of what keywords and phrases your prospects are using when they are looking for a company like yours. Some web developers are also experienced in SEO and can help you get your site noticed, while others are simply focused on creating your site. There are also companies that specialize solely on SEO – you bring them your site and they do the work to determine the best keywords and get your site to the top ranking. Of course, if

your site is developed using a CMS, there is no reason why you can't do this yourself and there are a number of resources available to help you out. It does take some time – to learn the basics, do some research on keywords and to execute your plan – so if you want someone else to handle that for you, be sure you discuss that with your web developer as well.

What Should I Know About My Domain?

If you have a website, you may be familiar with the process of selecting and registering your domain name. Your domain name is one way that your clients and prospects find you on the web, and it holds the routing information for your website, email and remote access to your company's resources.

Of course, you may have worked with a web site developer to select and register your name and left all of the details to them. That could turn out to be a mistake.

When a domain name is registered, information regarding the ownership of the domain is requested. This information falls into several categories from the name and address of the registrant to the administrative, technical and billing contacts.

It is critical that your company is listed as the registrant and that the address, phone number and email address are yours. Legally, the company listed as the registrant is the company that actually owns the domain. You should also have access to the login information for your domain registration in case it is ever needed.

The other contacts could contain your information, or they may contain information for the company that is responsible for setting up and maintaining your website and routing information.

I hear you now – "I don't know anything about setting up websites and I don't want to know. I just let my web guy handle all of that." Believe me I understand completely!

But business relationships sometimes go sour. Your web guy stops calling you back, or he goes out of business and leaves town without letting you know. Suddenly your website is down and your email isn't being delivered. You find someone else to help you figure this out and find out that the domain name has expired and it isn't listed as belonging to you.

At this point, you have two choices, both of which are bad:

1. Buy your domain name when it is released. This involves an auction and a 45 day wait from the time your domain expired. If your domain name is something that others would like to have, and they are bidding against you, this could be very expensive.
2. Pick a new domain name, register it and move your website to it. Of course, you no longer have access to the old site at this point because the domain expired, so if you don't have a backup copy of it, you may be recreating a web site.

Even when the domain is registered to you, if you do not know the log in for the account and you don't have access to the email address that was used to create it, the process to regain control is tedious and difficult.

One of our clients had registered their domain years ago. It had been done by an employee who used a personal email address for the registration. After all, at that point, you may not have a company email address to use for the contact information. As time went on, the situation changed and the employee was eventually fired. More time passed and the employee died. THEN the client needed to make changes to the domain. Of course, they didn't have the login information or access to the email address that was the only one listed in the contact information.

If that happens to you, you will need to contact the registrar (Network Solutions, GoDaddy, or similar) to have the information updated. You will need to prove that you represent the company or organization named as the registrant. This will involve providing legal documents such as incorporation papers, tax returns or similar, as well as proof of your identity and your legal authority as a representative of the organization. If there are differences between your legal name and the name on the domain registration, it may well be impossible for you to get control of the domain. Now you are back to the two undesirable options listed above.

As you might guess, this is not an easy process, and if you are forced to go through it, you will probably be extremely frustrated and impatient. But it is comforting to know that others can't easily have the information updated for purposes of taking your domain away from you!

Many technology companies are providing both network support and web services, so you may be dealing with the same company for both areas. In that case, you should ask them to show you the registration information for your domain and give you the user id and password to login to access the domain information. Of course, you can assure them that you won't change any of the information. Just explain to them that you know this is critical to your business and you want to be sure that you have access to the account. It is fine to have them listed as the technical contact for your domain so that they are also notified about expirations and periodic verification requests. A review of the registration information should be part of your annual technology review.

If you are dealing with different companies for network support and web services, they will both need access to the information. One of them will probably be responsible for making the necessary changes and the other one will request the changes. Perhaps the other one will review the registration information periodically to make sure that everything is in order.

What about Website Certificates?

Your technology company may tell you that you need to purchase a website or SSL certificate. And while you may think this is an expense that you can skip, if you are accessing corporate resources remotely, you should not accept the risks of not having a certificate.

SSL certificates provide for secure transactions between servers and browsers. If you are accessing your corporate email via a web browser, you want to be sure that the connection is secure to prevent interception of your login credentials. If a hacker were to intercept this information, it could be used to access your server, compromising your email account and documents.

If you are selling products online, the same type of certificates are used to protect confidential customer information such as names, addresses and credit card numbers. And if you are making purchases online, be sure that you check for the tiny yellow padlock somewhere in your web browser. Some browsers will display the padlock in the bottom right corner, while others will show it near the top of the window to the right of the address bar. You can also check the URL that is displayed. It should begin with "https" rather than the standard "http".

What are DNS entries and why are they important?

DNS stands for Domain Name Services and getting this right is critical for proper website access and email delivery.

You can think of DNS entries like a gigantic phone book for the internet. When someone attempts to access your website or send you an email, DNS entries are accessed to provide the necessary routing information. These entries are also used to correctly route traffic from employees who are working remotely.

DNS entries are generally created by the company that hosts your website and then replicated to other locations. When entries are changed, it can take as long as 48 hours for the changes to fully propagate. During that time, some users may be routed to the new locations, while others may still be routed to the old locations.

That's why it is critical that these entries are made correctly. If someone updates your DNS records with incorrect information and it fully propagates before the error is discovered, it can take 2 more days for the problem to be fully corrected.

Amazingly, we have run across many web developers who only understand how to correctly configure DNS entries for websites and have no understanding of how to correctly configure DNS for any other purpose. That's not a problem unless you turn control of your DNS over to them. We have seen instances where a new website was launched and hosted on a new server, immediately causing email and remote access to fail.

You don't need to understand all of the details of your DNS entries, but you absolutely need to understand that they affect much more than your website. If you decide to move your website and your DNS entries, you need to be absolutely sure that whoever is making the move knows all of the DNS entries that need to be made and that they are made correctly. If the new person gives you any indication that they are not sure what you are talking about, do not let them have control of your DNS entries. Your computer support company may well be more knowledgeable about what your DNS entries should be and, if so, they need to be in control of all changes made to them.

Viruses, Spyware and Hackers

I don't know of anything that causes more headaches than viruses, spyware, malware and the like. It seems that just when our defenses are in place to prevent one kind of attack a new one surfaces that is even more damaging than the ones before.

First a few definitions:

- A **virus** is a malicious program that attaches itself to another program or file with the intent of spreading or replicating itself. Some viruses cause only mildly annoying effects, while others can completely destroy your hardware, software and files. Almost all viruses are spread by executable files attached to an email. Unless you run or open the program, a virus cannot infect your computer. This is why you should NEVER open a strange-looking email from an unknown source.

- Like viruses, **worms** spread from computer to computer; but unlike a virus, a worm has the ability to take advantage of your computer's file or information transport feature to spread without human assistance. This is why worms are so dangerous. Left unchecked, a worm could send out thousands of copies of itself from your computer, creating a devastating ripple effect. For example, many worms will access your e-mail address book and send a copy of itself to everyone you have listed. If it is able to install itself on the recipient's machine, it performs the same broadcast to everyone in their e-mail address book, and so on down the line.
Because of the copying process they initiate, worms use up system memory and network bandwidth causing Web servers, network servers, and individual computers to stop responding. In some cases, like the Blaster Worm disaster, a worm can actually allow malicious users to control your computer remotely.

- A **Trojan**, named after the Trojan Horse of Greek mythology, received its name because of the way it tricks users into installing it on their computer. To an unsuspecting user, a trojan will appear to be useful software or files from a legitimate source. Once activated, the damage can be mildly annoying (like adding silly icons to your desktop) to outright devastating (deleting files and destroying information on your system).

  In addition to damaging files and destroying information, Trojans are known for creating an entry point that allows outsiders to access your system and possibly even steal confidential, financial, and personal information. Unlike viruses and worms, Trojans do not reproduce by infecting other files and do not self-replicate.

  Currently, there are a number of fake anti-virus Trojans in existence. These infections appear to be legitimate messages from anti-virus software companies. Not only do they easily trick users into installing malware, they follow up with promises of cleaning your system if you will purchase a paid subscription. The unwary user willingly provides credit card information to the criminals, and pays them $60 or so in the process. Of course, the computer remains infected and requires much work to restore normal operations.

Keeping your systems free from these types of infections must be a high priority. As wacky as it sounds, the infections that impact the performance of your system are probably much less dangerous than the unobtrusive trojan that is sending your information to cybercriminals without your knowledge. Ten years ago, hackers just wanted their spyware to make the news; the notoriety they gained was the payoff. Today, hackers are much more interested in profiting from their activities; the longer their malicious software is running on your machine, the more information they can steal.

Phishing

In response to better security that blocks threats before they reach the end user, the criminals only devise more ways to get around the security measures. Phishing refers to fraudulent attempts to acquire usernames, passwords, credit card and other information by posing as a trustworthy entity.

You have probably received emails from Nigeria requesting that you assist the sender in getting money out of Nigeria by allowing him to deposit the money in your account in the States and then withdraw most of it, leaving you with a generous percentage in payment. Of course, what really happens is that your account is simply emptied – no doubt resulting in money entering Nigeria rather than the reverse.

Of course, many schemes are much more subtle. You may receive an email that appears to have come from your bank or your credit card company requesting that you go to a website, link provided of course, to confirm your account credentials. Don't do it!

With the prevalence of social media sites and the wealth of information that is now available online, phishing schemes have become more sophisticated yet again. With just a few minutes of research, the criminals can find out names and email addresses of your co-workers and perhaps gain a bit of intelligence about projects you may be working on. With a little imagination and creativity, they can then craft an email message that appears to have come from your co-worker requesting specific information or requesting that you go to a website, link again thoughtfully provided, to get information that relates to the project. Of course, the link really installs malicious software on the unsuspecting user's workstation. Studies have shown that this type of phishing attack will succeed more than half the time.

You must train your employees to be very careful when clicking on links within email messages. A healthy dose of skepticism can go a long way towards protecting computers in your network. When in doubt, confirm the source of the message before taking any action.

How Do You Know If Your System has Been Infected?

Some infections are very hard to detect; that's why it is important that you have anti-virus and anti-spyware software installed on your systems. You also need to be sure that the definitions are updated and scans are run regularly. This is true even if your systems are sitting behind a rock solid firewall.

And you don't want to rely on free versions of anti-virus or anti-spyware software. While some free software has no restrictions, much of it is only free for residential users and using it in a commercial enterprise is against the free licensing agreement. In addition, free versions are never as robust as the paid versions.

Most spyware programs are designed to run undetected by the user, but there are warning signs like:

1. Your browser has been hijacked. If you open your Internet browser and a strange-looking homepage pops up and won't go away, chances are you have a spyware program installed on your computer. You may also discover that you cannot modify your browser settings and that your favorites folder has been modified.
2. You conduct a search, but another (unauthorized) browser completes it for you. For example, you type a search term into Microsoft IE, but another browser pops up and lists various web sites tied to your search term. This is a surefire sign of a spyware infection. You'll also notice that if you try to remove this program, it comes right back.
3. Your computer is unstable, sluggish, locks up, or crashes frequently. Spyware programs run in the background taking up memory and processor speed which will cause serious performance problems.
4. You constantly get pop-up ads displayed on your screen, even if you aren't browsing the Internet. Some of the ads may even be personalized with your name.

5. Mysterious files suddenly start appearing on your computer, your files are moved or deleted, or the icons on your desktop and toolbars are blank or missing.
6. You find e-mails in your "Sent Items" folder that you didn't send.

How Can I Protect My Company?

Here are 6 fundamentals:

1. Educate your users on security basics such as using strong passwords, and not downloading "cute" screen savers and illegal music. This should be covered in your Acceptable Use Policy mentioned earlier.
2. Make sure your firewall includes web filtering software to police users and prevent accidental (or intentional) slip-ups on the usage policies.
3. Install a good virus protection system on all computers on your network and maintain it. If you are entering into a managed services contract, make sure this is included and that the provider will remove any infections without additional charges.
4. Make sure your provider runs an intrusion test. This test will check for any security threats that may exist and provides information about how to resolve the issues. Make sure they share the results with you and remedy any vulnerabilities. If there are serious vulnerabilities, ask to have the report rerun to make sure everything has been corrected.
5. Keep all your servers updated with all the latest security patches. If you are in a contract that includes security updates, make sure your provider is actually doing this by asking for and reviewing periodic reports showing the number of patches installed during the reporting period.
6. Never keep any of the manufacturer's default settings on any of the appliances or software you install. Hackers know what these settings are and will use them to gain easy access to your network. This item nails more systems administrators than care to admit it.

Can Technology Help You Go Green?

Whether your motivation is to save the planet or save some money, going "green" with your office IT is a smart move. After all, who doesn't want to save a little money, especially when it's SO incredibly easy!

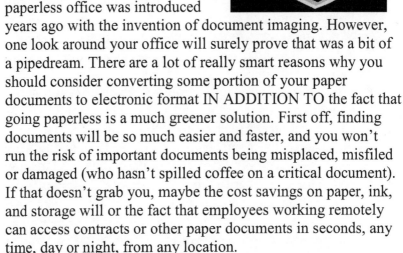

6 Ways to Go Green

1. **Go paperless!** The concept of the paperless office was introduced years ago with the invention of document imaging. However, one look around your office will surely prove that was a bit of a pipedream. There are a lot of really smart reasons why you should consider converting some portion of your paper documents to electronic format IN ADDITION TO the fact that going paperless is a much greener solution. First off, finding documents will be so much easier and faster, and you won't run the risk of important documents being misplaced, misfiled or damaged (who hasn't spilled coffee on a critical document). If that doesn't grab you, maybe the cost savings on paper, ink, and storage will or the fact that employees working remotely can access contracts or other paper documents in seconds, any time, day or night, from any location.

2. **Power down your network at night.** The computers in your office are the largest drain on electricity in your office; and considering you're only using them for approximately 9-10 hours a day, that means you're paying for 14-15 hours of unnecessary power. Intel vPro technology allows your systems to be powered down remotely and powered back up again in the morning without any interruption or interference with your systems' performance. This alone can save thousands on electricity. And if there is any maintenance to be done, it can still be done during off hours just before powering the systems down.

3. **Go virtual!** Depending on the exact implementation, virtualization can dramatically reduce the power requirements for servers and workstations alike. For more information on how virtualization fits into your efforts to go green, refer to the Virtualization chapter.

4. **Allow employees to work from home.** More and more businesses are creating virtual workspaces for several reasons. First, allowing employees to work from home perpetually or for a couple of days a week cuts down on gas and emissions. It's also a great retention strategy for your rock star employees. Additionally, allowing employees to work from home reduces the amount of office space needed, lowering or eliminating rent costs and utility bills. Finally, it's a great disaster preparedness plan. In the event of a fire or natural disaster, employees can keep the doors open by working remotely. For more information about working from home, refer to the chapter on Telecommuting and Remote Access.

5. **Choose new equipment wisely.** When you purchase new equipment, ask questions about its energy efficiency and the materials that are used to make it. If you haven't already, replace all of your old CRT monitors with new LCD monitors that use one third to one half less electricity. When buying new desktops, look for machines that have and 80+ rating for the power supply. This rating tells you that the power supply operates at 80 percent efficiency or higher, which can use as much as 10% less power. Major manufacturers will also offer systems that are EPEAT certified at various levels. Products that are RoHS (Restriction of Use of Hazardous Substances) compliant have undergone testing to verify that certain substances are reduced or eliminated, thus reducing the environmental impact of these products.

6. **Dispose of old electronics responsibly.** Your computer is made with a wide variety of components, many of which are toxic. When old computers are disposed of improperly, these substances can enter the environment, causing pollution and associated plant and animal death, along with birth defects.

Many of these components are also produced in unsustainable ways, causing even more environmental harm. Because these components can be recovered and recycled, throwing out an old computer is simply irresponsible. If you have old equipment, you can often donate it to a charity for a tax break. Not only will that solve the disposal problem, but you'll save a little money too!

Power Protection

Most of us take power for granted. We walk into a room, flip the switch and have instant light. Many of us leave our computers running 24 hours a day, plugged directly into the wall and don't give the quality and consistency of the power a second thought, at least until there is a power failure or an intense thunderstorm rolls through.

Storms can definitely cause problems due to lightning strikes and power outages. Certainly you can watch the weather and when it turns nasty, you can shut everything down and unplug it all to protect it. But that's a lot of work and what if the storms come during the night when you aren't near that expensive server? And don't forget that your office has 20 or 30 workstations and, while each one is probably worth something under $1000, when you add up the total value, it's a pretty big number.

A much better approach is to make sure every piece of equipment is protected against power problems. You may not be aware that there are many power problems present even when there isn't a storm and that these problems can be just as damaging as what you may experience during a storm.

Types of Power Disturbances

Power surges are an increase in the voltage that powers electrical equipment. Surges often go unnoticed; often they are quick (1/20th of a second) and absorbed by the power supply of a device. Stronger surges will go through a power supply, damaging any circuits as it moves along the grounding line.

Surges come from utility power systems that have become unstable or unreliable. Power grids often generate surges as they switch between sources to generate power. Local surges can occur when power is suddenly added or taken away from a local area. Good examples are if someone starts up an electrical motor or a fuse blows.

In the case of a fuse blowing, for a moment there will be more power available to the rest of a house. This sudden excess power can cause a surge.

Lightning can send a spectacular power surge along any conductive line. This is more than just a standard surge - no surge suppressor in the world will survive a direct lightning strike. By choosing the right power protection, your surge suppressor will take the hit, end up melted, but your equipment will stay protected. Don't forget that telephone lines are also highly conductive.

Brownouts are periods of low voltage in utility lines that can cause lights to dim and equipment to fail. Also known as voltage sags, this is the most common power problem, accounting for up to 87% of all power disturbances. Brownouts can also be caused by damaged electrical lines, or equipment that draws massive amounts of power, such as hair dryers, refrigerators, air conditioners or laser printers.

When line voltages are lowered, electrical equipment pulls more current to compensate and generates more heat in the process. Over time, this can contribute to equipment failure.

Brownouts are often caused when utility companies must reduce their voltage output to deal with demands for power that exceed the supply of power. Brownouts are also referred to as undervoltages; there is power, just not enough to meet the demand of equipment using it. Brownouts place undue strain on power supplies and other internal components, forcing them to work harder in order to function. Extended brownouts can destroy electrical components and cause data glitches and hardware failure.

Undervoltages are often followed by **overvoltages** or s**pikes**, which are also damaging to computer components and data. Voltage variation can be the most damaging power problem to threaten your equipment. All electronic devices expect to receive a steady voltage (120 VAC in North America and 220/240 volts in many other parts of the world) in order to operate correctly.

Overvoltages burn out power supplies and other components and can cause massive damage to electronic hardware. Extended overvoltages can even cause fires as electronics "fry" in the extra electricity.

Blackouts or **power failures** are the easiest power problem to diagnose. Any temporary, or not so temporary, interruption in the flow of electricity will result in a power failure which can cause hardware damage and data loss.

Blackouts can be caused by many things - weather, overburdened power grids, or the severing of a power line. Power failures are more than simply inconvenient and annoying. Because most computers use a volatile storage method (writing to memory prior to saving on to a hard-drive), information is lost when power is removed. Data can become corrupted, and some devices can be damaged by the sudden loss of power. When the power comes back, spikes can occur that may cause even more damage.

Line noise refers to random fluctuations - electrical impulses that are carried along with standard AC current. Turning on the fluorescent lights overhead, a refrigerator, laser printers, working near a radio station, using a power generator, or simply working during a lightning storm can all introduce line noise into computer systems.

Line noise interference can result in many different symptoms depending on the particular situation. Noise can introduce glitches and errors into programs and files. Hard drive components can be damaged. Televisions and computer monitors can display interference as "static" or "snow," and audio systems experience increased distortion levels. Noise suppression is stated as Decibel level (Db) at a specific frequency (KHz or MHz). The higher the Db, the greater the protection.

Protection from Power Disturbances

If you want to be sure that your equipment keeps running during an outage, you will want to invest in an uninterruptible power supply or UPS. These devices also protect against fluctuations in power levels by delivering consistent power to equipment. Power sags are boosted and spikes are absorbed.

To select the right UPS, you will need to determine how much power will be drawn and how long you need your systems to run during an outage. You can purchase UPS systems that will run your system for an hour or longer, or you can provide for just enough runtime to safely shutdown the equipment. Software provided with most UPS systems will monitor the utility power and perform a shutdown based on parameters you provide. Obviously, the longer runtime you need the more you will spend on the UPS.

If you decide that you would like for your server to continue running for an hour, perhaps because you have staff that works remotely or your server processes email and you want that function to continue, don't forget to consider that you may need some of your networking equipment to continue running as well. For remote access and email, you will need your firewall, router and switches, as well as your server to remain powered.

Workstations should also be protected against power problems. A small UPS will do the job nicely and monitor utility power. Workstations will not reboot when the lights flicker, and if there is a power outage of any duration, the workstations will be automatically shutdown, preventing loss of data and damage to the operating system files. Expect to pay $60 for a UPS that will run just long enough to power your system down – assuming that you aren't powering your monitor or any other peripherals. If you want to be able to use the workstation for a time during a power outage, you will need to connect your monitor to the battery as well, and the unit will be more expensive.

For peripheral equipment, like switches and monitors, protection can be provided with a high quality surge suppressor or voltage regulator. Don't think that a $10 or $15 surge suppressor will provide adequate protection. Look for one that offers an equipment protection policy. These policies will pay for damaged equipment in the event that the device fails to protect it. Policies may cover as much at $25,000. Expect to pay $25 to $50 for most applications.

Keeping Your Computer Clean

Many of the questions I get from our clients have to do with how to keep their computers clean. While some aspects of keeping your computer clean are purely cosmetic, keeping your computer free of dust can extend the life of your system.

Eliminating a Little Known Threat to Computers and Servers

We generally think of viruses, spyware, or hackers when considering computer threats, but one that is often overlooked is heat; and it can be one of the most sinister enemies of electronics and computer equipment. Here are a few simple ways for you to reduce or eliminate this threat and keep your computer safe from damaging heat:

Take Off the "Dust Quilt" – No matter how clean your home or office, dust eventually accumulates in hard to reach places like your computer circuit board or processor. The cooling ventilation fan sucks the dust into the case, and the magnetic field created by the computer components acts like dust "glue." We recommend opening up your computer to remove dust buildup at least once a year, twice if you are in a dusty environment or if you have pets in your home or office. Just make sure you power the machine off and use an approved computer vacuum so you don't damage your PC.

Check The Circulation – While you have the computer cover off, clear off the dust bunnies in the exhaust vent. The cooling fan will lose 50% efficiency or more if airflow is restricted. Next, check the cooling fan by spinning it with your finger. It should spin easily and freely.

Make A Gap – Many people put their computers on the floor, in hidden cabinets, or in other tight spaces with little or no clearance. It certainly makes sense organizationally, but these places can restrict air flow causing excess heat and dust buildup in the computer box.

Make Sure Your Computer Room Is Cool – The room where you store your server should have its own ventilation and, ideally, its own temperate control. If possible, keep the room slightly cooler than room temperature (68 degrees) and close the door to keep out dust.

Laptop Trick – Laptops are jam packed with tiny components that can easily overheat. Although most are equipped with cooling fans, they aren't designed to run constantly. To keep it from overheating, place it on an old fashioned baker's cooling rack. This will keep airflow underneath moving and your laptop cool!

How Can I Clean My Flat Screen Monitor Safely?

Although each monitor manufacturer has its own special instructions for cleaning, there are some common guidelines you can use to get your screen looking like new in no time.

- **Turn off the monitor**. It's not required, but it makes smudges and smears easier to see.
- **Use a cotton cloth** or compressed air to get rid of light dust buildup. Never use a rag or paper towel to clean since they can scratch the screen.
- **Don't use products with ethyl alcohol or ammonia based products**. Products like Windex can yellow flat-screen or laptop monitors.
- **Use water or a homemade mix to clean grungy surfaces**. If water is not enough, concoct a cleaning solution of 1 part water, 1 part isopropyl alcohol, and 1/2 part vinegar.
- **Lightly moisten your cloth with the cleaning solution**. Never apply the liquid directly to the screen.
- **Wipe the cloth in one direction** – from top to bottom. This method will ensure grime and dust move to the bottom of the screen surface where it can be wiped away.

One final guideline, never touch or press on your LCD screen with your fingers as this can cause the pixels to burn out.

Three Easy Steps to Get More Life Out of Your Laser Printer

Printers - the necessary evil of every office. From paper jams and error messages, to problems like smearing, misfeeds, and ghosting, printers can really make your blood pressure rise.

Plus, it's easy to sink thousands of dollars into maintenance and repairs. If you want to avoid common printer problems AND save yourself a small fortune on replacements and repairs, follow these three easy steps.

Keep It Clean – There is no faster way to gunk up a laser printer and cause printing problems than by letting it get dirty.

On a monthly basis, use compressed air to blow out the inside of the printer. Remove the toner cartridge for better access, and don't forget to do the back if it is accessible. It also helps to take a vacuum to the outside. If you print labels or use any other type of specialty media like transparencies, use rubbing alcohol to clean the rollers inside the printer.

Perform Regular Maintenance – You can almost infinitely extend your printer's lifespan by doing the regular maintenance suggested by the manufacturer.

This includes replacing rollers, filters, and occasionally replacing the fuser (the printer's internal furnace.) Here's a little money-saving secret: you only need to do this type of maintenance at 1.5 to 2 times the manufacturer's usage recommendation. In other words, if your printer's manufacturer says to replace rollers every 100,000 pages, you really only need to do so every 150,000 to 200,000 pages. Of course, some manufacturers shut down the printer when a part needs to be replaced and will not function until it is replaced.

Use a Surge Protector – Nothing will send your printer to the bone yard faster than an electrical surge caused by lightning or other issues on the power grid. When internal components are fried, it is often cheaper to buy a new printer than it is to fix the existing one. It is easy to protect yourself with a $25 surge protector. DO NOT plug a laser printer into a UPS or other battery backup system. The printer's power draw is too much for a battery to handle.

Dealing with Cell Phones

Cell phones have become an essential business tool for anyone with sales staff or providing services outside their own office. When everything is working properly, they are an indispensable tool, tracking email, contacts, tasks and calendars by synchronizing with the same corporate systems that are used in the office.

Which cell phone to use is largely a matter of personal preference. You probably know people who wouldn't give up their iPhone for anything, others that swear by their BlackBerry, and a few who have one of the new (as of this writing) Android phones. Less popular, but with similar capabilities, are the Palm models. Now before someone screams that none of the Palms have similar capabilities to the iPhone, let me qualify that by saying that I am speaking here ONLY about the phones ability to sync critical business information!

While all of these phones have the ability to sync email, contacts and calendar information, there are some differences in how it is done.

First, you need to understand that if you want to sync information 'on the go', you will need to have a mail server that handles your email, calendar and contacts. The most common mail server that has these capabilities is Microsoft Exchange, although there are others. Without such a mail server, the only way you can sync your phone with the calendar and contacts on your computer is to physically tether your phone to your workstation.

You can receive email without a mail server, but there are some differences in how the synchronization works. Without a mail server, there will be no communication back from your phone to your mail server. So if you open a message, read it and delete it, you will see it again when you access your email on your workstation. If you are using Exchange, actions taken on messages from your phone are updated back to the mail server, making it much easier to determine which messages you have read and responded to while on the road.

If you are using Exchange and want full featured synchronization with your phones, you need to know that the BlackBerry does not synchronize with Exchange natively. You must have some additional software, BlackBerry Enterprise Server, to enable synchronization. Typically, your cell phone provider will offer you a free copy of the software with an initial number of licenses. As you add additional phones, you will need to purchase additional licenses, AND you need to be sure that the phone itself is enrolled in the enterprise plan.

With the iPhone, Android phones and Palm phones, synchronization is simply a matter of configuring the proper account settings to access your email server. No additional software will be required.

If you are talking to a cell phone carrier, be very cautious if they brush off your concerns about synchronization. Remember that they make money by selling you the phone and the service. Synchronizing will be your problem.

Better yet, ask your technology company to help you make the right choice for your business. They should also be able and willing to help you set up the phones once you have them and deal with any issues you have with the carrier.

Social Media

This chapter could easily be an entire book by itself. Indeed, there are many that are much more savvy with social media than I am that have written excellent books on this subject.

Social media refers to any web based technology that allows and promotes interaction between members of a community. Examples of 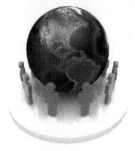 social media sites include LinkedIn, Facebook, Twitter, MySpace, Flikr and many, many others.

Social networking isn't new. In years past, you probably attended a variety of networking events – after hour mixers or business luncheons and breakfasts, for example. You may have even joined several organizations with the expectations that you would become acquainted with other business owners or people who share similar interests.

Social media sites are very similar in that they allow you to make those same kinds of connections. The difference is that you meet people in a virtual world which may lead to a face to face meeting. Technology makes it possible to meet more people more quickly and to identify the people you want to connect with more easily.

According to a study conducted by Nielsen Online, the time spent last year reading our friends' Facebook Updates and sharing "25 Random Things About Me" questionnaires totaled 1.7 billion minutes. That's a 700% increase in time spent virtually loafing around online. Additionally, Twitter saw a 3,712% year-over-year increase between last and this year, with users clocking in nearly 300,000 total minutes for that site in April 2009.

While these sites were primarily used by young people 3 years ago, the number of people 55 and over that are joining is growing faster than any other demographic. According to iStrategyLabs, the number of Facebook users over 55 in the US grew by over 900% between January 2009 and January 2010.

Perhaps one of the major differences between younger users of these sites and those of us who are older is that younger people tend to look at these sites as THE way they communicate and gather information. Those of us who are older add these sites to the ways that we already receive information. We may read the local paper and watch the local news in addition to time spent on Facebook. Our younger friends rely on members of their online communities to post links to interesting information or breaking news.

So which sites should you be paying attention to and participating in? The answers depend a bit on what business you are in and what connections you want to make.

My first exposure to social media was through LinkedIn, www.linkedin.com. This site was started in 2002 to facilitate professional networking. Consequently, it is a great place to be if you are marketing to businesses. Even if you are consumer oriented, it can be a great resource to locate professionals who provide services that you need or look for professionals to fill job openings that you may have.

Your LinkedIn profile should include a professional photo and details about your background – current and previous positions, as well as your education and training. You can also include links to your company website, and two additional websites. If you have more than one company, or more than one website for your company, list them! If you have a blog, you probably want to use one of the website links for it. You can also list your twitter account in a separate area. Don't forget to include a few of your interests outside of work.

Once your profile is set up, invitations can be sent to your colleagues and connections established. You can also recommend people you have worked with or worked for and request that others do the same for you. You also have the opportunity to update your status to let your connections know what you are working on.

I recommend that you also create a listing for your company and ask any of your professional employees to join and complete their profiles as well. While you may have some of this information on your company website, it never hurts to have the information in more than one place, and if your prospects meet one of your employees, you want to be sure that they will be able to find you from them!

You will also have the ability to create events and invite people to attend, post job openings, join special interest groups and even create your own groups for others to join. You can also ask questions and answer questions about your area of expertise. Your participation in this area can help position you as an expert in a particular area.

LinkedIn has excellent search capabilities allowing you to identify companies that you would like to work with and the people who work there. Once you have gotten that far, you can easily see if you know people who know them and can make an introduction. You can also review their profiles to see if they may have a connection to you – perhaps you attended the same college 10 years apart, or worked for the same company but never met there. This type of intelligence can serve as an excellent ice breaker and help you establish rapport much more quickly than you would otherwise be able to.

Facebook, www.facebook.com, and MySpace, www.myspace.com, are much more personal in nature. Facebook was started to allow college students to communicate and MySpace has been quite popular with musicians. I don't use MySpace and I don't know many people who do, but I know many who use Facebook.

Facebook lets you post pictures and interact with your friends in too many ways to detail. You can comment on your friends' pictures and tag them in yours. Wall-to-wall provides a way to communicate publicly, but on each wall, you see only one side of the conversation – which is sometimes really baffling! You can link to your websites and post links to other articles, videos and a myriad of other information. Facebook also has an easily updatable status and it can be updated via cell phone and through other websites. Many people update their status information several times a day, while others update much less frequently.

If your kids have a Facebook page, I recommend that you setup a page of your own and friend them. Be aware that it is possible to share information with all of your friends except a specific friend, so it might be a good idea to look at their page with them from time to time. My own kids are 27 and 29 and we are Facebook friends. I am also friends with my nieces who are 16 and 19 and I check their pages regularly. I think it is good for them to know that an adult is looking over their shoulder, and I know them in a way that I would not otherwise. (They live in Illinois and I see them only a few times a year.) I am also friends with a number of people in my husband's family and it is easy to keep up with all of them – and should make those family reunions a lot more fun. We will already have things to talk about!

Some people decide that they will only be Facebook friends with people that are personal friends. While this is a decision that may well be the right one for some people, I am friends with a number of people who are business contacts. Many of them are also connections in LinkedIn. But I learn so much more about them on Facebook! Statuses on Facebook are more likely to be personal in nature, although work does pop up regularly as well.

You can also setup a Facebook page for your business where you can post news and photos, as well as engage your clients and customers in a dialogue. Facebook will track some demographic information about your fans and send you weekly reports about activity on your page.

So how do you leverage Facebook if you are marketing to businesses? Imagine that you have met someone whose business is complimentary to yours and you can envision a partnership of some sort. But you really don't know who this person is. Of course, you can always meet for coffee or lunch, and that is a great start. But if you follow that up by establishing a friend relationship on Facebook, you suddenly know what that person likes to do, read and watch. If they update their status regularly and their friends write on their wall, you can get a pretty good idea of whether or not this person is someone that you want to be associated with. And you may find that you have common interests on which you can build a friendship and a business relationship.

Above all, remember that the information you post is at least somewhat public. Review your privacy settings so you know who can view your information. Remember too, that your friends and connections can likely see some information about your other friends and don't be afraid to break a friendship or connection if someone is posting things that you wouldn't want on your own profile.

Twitter also began with college students who have been using it to keep in touch with friends. Many, many people use twitter exclusively from their cell phones – no computer required! If you are out for the evening and hoping to find your friends, you can simply broadcast where you are and wait for your friends to respond. For that reason, twitter is a great place to promote your coffee shop, restaurant or other consumer focused business.

My first exposure to twitter came when I heard it mentioned during the 2008 Presidential campaign. I spent a bit of time trying to figure it out, but it seemed really strange, so I forgot about it. Next I started seeing baffling entries in a friend's facebook statuses. Things like @jmcw or #troppo. I had no idea what he was talking about, but of course I didn't want to ask!

Then it started to become clear when that same friend, Ryan Doom of Web Ascender, posted a blog entry titled "What is Twitter, why should I use it?". He gave an overview similar to what I have already told you here, and told a story about how he managed to meet up with a friend at a concert through twitter, even though neither of them knew that the other one would be there.

I still wasn't convinced that I wanted to spend any time tweeting, so I pretty much ignored twitter – that is until one of my coaches started an account and asked us to follow her. So, I set up my account and started following her and some of my friends that were already following her. Of course, I also started following Ryan and a few other people that I happened to run across.

Initially, I kept my group of twitter friends somewhat small, following mostly people in my industry, and a few assorted people that I just found interesting. I was constantly surprised by the fact that someone would start following me out of the blue - and I couldn't figure out any way that we were connected in reality. Some of these people I followed in return, but not always.

One of my first surprises came after I tweeted about my weekly Rotary meeting. Within about an hour, I was being followed by Rotary International. A few weeks later, our meeting topic was a presentation from one of our older members who spoke on what Rotary meant to him. So I tweeted "What does Rotary mean to you?" and got two responses from people in other parts of the country. This happened because Rotary International distributed my tweet via a re-tweet – broadcasting my message to all of their followers.

If you spend some time checking out twitter, you will discover a number of people who are just letting the world know what they are doing. Others use their tweets to post links to articles they have written, blog posts, or other web pages with their information. Some of this is just another way to make online marketing work. Others post information about breaking news, with links to more information.

Somewhere in my journey, I started looking for people in the Lansing area to follow on twitter. You see, one of the big differences between twitter and the other sites is that you don't have to know someone to follow them. While it is possible to restrict your tweets so that they can only be viewed by people you allow to follow you, most people don't do that. This tactic has not only broadened my online network, I have met many of these people in person. It is quite unlikely that I would have met most of them without social media.

I have also connected with various people in other parts of the world. On a trip to Indonesia, a local man read my tweeted observations of my trip, commented and we became friends. Although I did not meet him in person, we have continued to correspond via twitter, email and facebook. I consider him to be a friend and hope that perhaps we will meet in the future.

So how does this affect you as a business owner? For one, if you are using it for marketing purposes, it may be GOOD news, especially if social media junkies are spending some of their time reading your Twitter posts or becoming fans of your Facebook page. However, if your employees are spending hours online chatting with their friends or goofing off, it can mean thousands of dollars in lost productivity. A few years back, employers would install security cameras and time clocks to make sure employees weren't goofing off, stealing paper towels or sleeping at their desks; nowadays, these threats seems minor compared to the damage a disgruntled or less-than-ethical employee can do to you online.

Here are a few thoughts regarding social media and your employees.

1. Have a signed social media policy in place for your employees – and enforce it. This should be added to your acceptable use policy. Intel Corporation has a very well thought out social media policy and you can find it online by searching for "Intel Social Media Guidelines".

2. Sign up for "Google Alerts" on your company at www.google.com/alerts. This service will send you an e-mail alert whenever someone posts something regarding a keyword you specify. We recommend setting up alerts for your name and company name at a minimum.

3. Install and use content filtering software for all employee PCs. This will automatically police employees' online usage and enforce your policies.

Above all, if you have concerns about how your employees are using their time online, be sure to discuss it with your technology provider. A good firewall can give you reports that show you how they are using their time and help you maintain control.

Glossary

While I have attempted to explain terms and acronyms in this book and not make things too technical, that's not completely possible. In some places, I wanted to present information without explaining every technical term, or the term may be used before it was explained. So, I have included this glossary in an attempt to provide additional explanation for those terms and concepts.

AUP – Acceptable Use Policy. Document that outlines how employees can – and can't – use company email, Internet and other electronic media.

Backup – The process of making a duplicate copy of data and programs so that they can be restored if necessary.

Business Continuity – Activities performed by a business to insure that critical business functions will continue in the event of a natural or human induced disaster. Business continuity planning includes development of plans, policies, guidelines and policies to restore interrupted functions as quickly as possible.

Disaster Recovery – Process, policies and procedures related to restoring normal operations after a natural or human induced disaster.

End Point Security – Concept that assumes each device, called an end point, is responsible for its own security. End points may be desktops, notebooks or servers. This type of security is important to protect against threats that may be brought into the office by employees via USB drives, CDs or DVDs.

Exchange – Microsoft Exchange Server. Server software that provides email, calendaring, contacts and tasks, as well as mobile and web-based access to information.

Firewall - A firewall prevents unauthorized access to a private network. A firewall can be implemented using either hardware or software, or a combination of both.

Gateway – A gateway is the device that provides access between computer networks. In your business network, the gateway is the device that provides access to the internet from your internal network or LAN. Gateway services are typically provided by a router.

HaaS – Hardware as a Service. An agreement that provides necessary hardware for a monthly fee rather than a lump sum fee. Typically, the hardware remains the property of the company that provides the equipment.

LAN – Local Area Network. A LAN connects computers that are geographically close together in the same office or building. Generally speaking, the connection is made through the use of cables that are run from a central location to each workstation. Connections can also be made wirelessly in cases where running cables is not practical, notebooks are present and move around the office frequently, or to provide guest access for visitors.

Phishing – The criminally fraudulent process of attempting to acquire sensitive information such as usernames, passwords and credit card details by masquerading as a trustworthy entity in an electronic communication.

SaaS – Software as a Service. SaaS is a model that eliminates upfront purchase of software in favor of a monthly fee that allows use of the software. The software actually runs in a data center and is accessed through the internet. This model makes advanced software more affordable for small businesses and reduces the need for resources in your office.

SQL Database – Often pronounced like "sequel". SQL stands for Structured Query Language, a database computer language for managing data in a database. Many applications rely on SQL services to provide backend data management.

TaaS – Technology as a Service. An agreement that provides all hardware, software and services for a monthly fee. The alternative to a TaaS agreement is to purchase the equipment and enter into an agreement for the services required to keep everything running smoothly.

UTM – Unified Threat Management. A comprehensive security solution that builds upon an organization's firewall. In addition to preventing unauthorized access, a firewall product that provides UTM will block specific types of content on the Internet, such as pornography or gambling, as well as monitoring network traffic, and preventing spam and viruses from entering the network.

VDI – Virtual Desktop Infrastructure. VDI refers to the necessary hardware and software required on the server to support virtual desktops.

Virtual CIO – Virtual Chief Information Officer. CIO is the job title commonly given to the most senior executive in an enterprise responsible for the information technology and computer systems that support the enterprise goals. The CIO typically reports to the CEO or CFO. A Virtual CIO is a part time consultant who assists small businesses who do not need a full time CIO. The virtual CIO advises the business owner regarding technology, but has generally has no day to day responsibility for managing the operation. When virtual CIO services are provided under a managed services agreement, the virtual CIO likely manages the team that provides day to day technology support.

VoIP – Voice over IP – The ability to run voice calls over the Internet.

VPN – Virtual Private Network. A VPN is a form of communication over networks that are public in ownership, but emulate a private network in terms of security. A VPN may be implemented using hardware, usually when two offices each with multiple systems are connecting, or using software when one remote system is connecting to a main location. A hardware solution would also be used when an office with multiple systems is connecting to a server that is located elsewhere, typically a data center.

WAN - Wide Area Network. A WAN connects LANs to each other and offers the means to provide services and resources in multiple locations. Most organizations rely on an internet service provider to provide a WAN, although if an organization has two locations that are close together, WAN services may be provided via a point to point connection.

Acknowledgements

When I first began this book, it seemed overwhelming. How could I ever narrow down such a huge subject to just the basics and explain them in a way that wouldn't completely overwhelm those who don't work, live and breathe technology? I am grateful for those who read what I had written and gave me feedback. Your comments have helped me make this book more complete and clear than it would have been otherwise.

I am grateful to several members of the John Dodge CEO Group – Wendell Parsons, CEO of Stamprite Supersine; Rudy Hirt, President of TMN Builders; Chuck Levy, President of Shinberg Insurance Services; Jeanne Rutledge, President of Medical Management Systems of Michigan, Inc. Their review of my manuscript and feedback was very valuable and insured that the book would be understandable to someone who does not have a technology background.

Special thanks to Ryan Doom, CEO of Web Ascender. Ryan is also in my CEO group, but more importantly is a friend who has helped me understand the world of web design and social media. He probably doesn't think he deserves any credit for that, but he has never failed to point me in the right direction and answer my questions.

My network support team at KI Technology Group, Aaron Meadows, Adam Meadows and Jon Mogle, made certain that I had all of the technical details correct, as they do nearly every day. I appreciate the time they spent explaining some of the more technical points in terms that I understood and answering question after question until I was sure I could explain things in layman's terms.

Special thanks to Craig Allen of Adventyx for reviewing the information about phone systems. His expertise in this area is far beyond mine!

It was also a great privilege to have my book reviewed by my good friend and peer, David Snell. David and his wife, Pam, have become good friends through our participation with Robin Robins and

Technology Marketing Toolkit. His offer to review it for me and his willingness to write the foreword is a great compliment.

Thanks to MJ Shoer of Jenaly Technology Group in Portsmouth, New Hampshire. I can't quite remember where I first met MJ, but we have known each other for several years. He has taught me so much about how to run my business and has been a terrific example as I have worked on improving my own business. His encouragement on this project and so many others is much appreciated.

Fred Reck from InnoTek Computer Consulting in Northeast Pennsylvania is another peer who was willing to review and provide comments. Thanks Fred!

Robin Robins has provided encouragement, ideas and occasional cajoling as I have worked on marketing and growing my company. Without her wise counsel and emphasis on accountability, I would not have achieved nearly what I have.

My business partner, Roger Robertson, provided not only expert proofreading and feedback on the clarity of the content, but also works tirelessly to keep our books in order. We have worked together for 24 years and seem to have finally hit on the way to really make our company work.

Lastly, very little of what I do would be possible without the love and support of my husband, John. He puts up with my crazy work habits, (it is my habit to work when I am awake) and makes sure there is food on our table and a roof over our heads. He has made the last 24 years of my life a lot more fun and allowed me to be much more successful than I would have imagined. Without him, I would truly be lost!

About the Author

Linda Lynch graduated from Michigan State University in 1979 with a Bachelors of Science in Computer Science. A computer programmer by training, she held programming positions at Consumers' Energy and Burroughs Corporation before coming to KI Technology Group in 1986.

At KI Technology Group, Linda has handled most aspects of supporting and training clients and acquired an ownership interest in the company in 1990 and has been serving as President since 1992. She has also been instrumental in managing the company's transition from a software company to a full service technology company, providing outsourced IT services to businesses in the greater Lansing area.

Linda participates in a number of industry organizations, including The ASCII Group and CompTIA, where she has served on the Solution Provider Education Committee. Participation in conferences and regional meetings held by these organizations and select vendors help Linda stay current on trends in the industry and best practices for technology companies.

Locally, Linda has been a member of the Career Quest Advisory Council since 2004 and is a member of the Capital Area IT Council. She was recently elected to the Board of Capital Area United Way and is a member of their Communications Committee. She is also a member of the Rotary Club of Lansing and the Founding Chapter of the National Association of Career Women, where she will assume the role of Vice-President for the 2010-2011 term.

In her spare time, Linda enjoys golfing, reading and playing electric bass in the Saturday night worship band at her church. She also enjoys vacationing with her husband of 23 years, John. Together they have taken nearly 20 cruises and visited many exciting ports.

Linda and her husband, John, have lived in Dansville, Michigan for 20 years, where they enjoy country life and fresh eggs from their small flock of chickens.

You can contact Linda online or by phone or mail:

Email:	linda@KITechnologyGroup.com
Twitter:	www.twitter.com/ljlynch
Facebook:	www.facebook.com/linda.j.lynch
LinkedIn:	www.linkedin.com/in/ljlynch
Phone:	517-333-6540
Mail:	KI Technology Group 4750 S Hagadorn Rd Ste 20 East Lansing, MI 48823
Website:	www.KITechnologyGroup.com